FOOD LOVERS

ASIAN

FOOD LOVERS

ASIAN

RECIPES SELECTED BY MARIE CLAYTON

Trans Atlantic Press

All recipes serve four people, unless otherwise indicated.

For best results when cooking the recipes in this book, buy fresh ingredients and follow the instructions carefully. Make sure that everything is properly cooked through before serving, particularly any meat and shellfish, and note that as a general rule vulnerable groups such as the very young, elderly people and pregnant women should avoid dishes that contain raw eggs. Take care when cooking with chilies, If slicing or chopping chilies, it is a wise precaution to wear disposable plastic gloves. Take care not to touch your eyes if you have been handling chilies.

For all recipes, quantities are given in standard U.S. cups and imperial measures, followed by the metric equivalent. Follow one set or the other, but not a mixture of both because conversions may not be exact. Standard spoon and cup measurements are level and are based on the following:

1 tsp = 5 ml, 1 tbsp = 15 ml, 1 cup = 250 ml / 8 fl oz.

Note that Australian standard tablespoons are 20 ml, so Australian readers should use 3 tsp in place of 1 tbsp when measuring small quantities.

The electric oven temperatures in this book are given for conventional ovens with top and bottom heat. When using a fan oven, the temperature should be decreased by about 20–40°F / 10–20°C – check the oven manufacturer's instruction book for further guidance.

CONTENTS

SOUPS

CREAMY BLACK BEAN SOUP

Ingredients

2 tbsp oil

1 onion, chopped

2 garlic cloves, crushed

Thumb-size piece fresh ginger, peeled and grated

1 tsp ground cumin

½ tsp ground curcuma (turmeric)

3½ cups / 800 ml vegetable broth (stock)

2 tbsp tomato paste (purée)

1 lb 6 oz / 600 g canned black beans, drained and rinsed

Scant 1 cup / 200 ml light (single) cream

1 tbsp balsamic vinegar

4 tbsp yogurt, to garnish

Salt and pepper

Dill sprigs, to garnish

Method

Prep and cook time: 45 min

1. Heat the oil in a large pan, add the onion and garlic and fry until soft but not brown.

2. Add the ginger, cumin and curcuma (turmeric) and fry for 30 seconds then pour in the broth (stock).

3. Add the tomato paste (purée) and beans. Bring to a boil, season with salt and pepper, then turn down the heat and simmer for 30 minutes.

4. Take out half of the beans, purée the soup, then put the beans back into the soup. Stir in the cream, reheat the soup and add the vinegar. If the soup is too thick, stir in a little water.

5. Ladle into bowls, add a swirl of yogurt to each and garnish with dill.

HOT AND SOUR SOUP WITH PORK

Ingredients

2 tbsp sesame oil

1 lb / 450 g pork loin, sliced into matchsticks

2 chili peppers, seeded and finely chopped (wear gloves to prevent irritation)

1 inch / 3 cm fresh ginger root, peeled and grated

3½ cups / 800 ml strong chicken broth (stock)

3 tbsp rice vinegar

7 oz / 200 g preserved Mu Err mushrooms, finely sliced*

Soy sauce, to taste

2 tbsp chopped cilantro (fresh coriander) leaves, to garnish

Method

Prep and cook time: 40 min

1. Heat the oil in a skillet or wok. Add the pork and stir-fry until no longer pink, about 1 minute. Transfer to a plate and return the skillet to the heat.

2. Add the ginger and chilies and stir-fry 1 minute, then add the broth (stock), vinegar and mushrooms and simmer for around 20 minutes.

3. Return the pork and its juices to the soup. Season with soy sauce and serve, sprinkled with cilantro (coriander).

*Preserved Mu Err (wood ear) mushrooms can be found in Asian markets. If unavailable substitute sliced fresh shiitake mushrooms.

CHICKEN SOUP WITH BEAN SPROUTS

Ingredients

For the curry paste:

1 chili

1 shallot

½ tsp chopped lemongrass

1 tsp freshly grated ginger

Good pinch cumin

1 tsp ground curcuma (turmeric)

For the soup:

14 oz / 400 g chicken breast fillet

2 garlic cloves

¾ inch / 2-cm piece of fresh ginger

1 stalk lemongrass

2 tbsp oil

1½ cups / 200 g soybean sprouts

1¾ cups / 400 ml chicken broth (stock)

1¾ cups / 400 ml unsweetened coconut milk

2 tbsp lime juice

2 tbsp fish sauce

Fresh mint leaves, to garnish

Method
Prep and cook time: 30 min

1. Put all the curry paste ingredients into a mortar and grind to a paste.

2. Poach the chicken in simmering salted water for 5–8 minutes. Take out of the water and let drain. Tear the meat into pieces in the direction of the grain.

3. Peel and finely chop the garlic and ginger. Crush the lemongrass. Heat the oil in a wok. Put the meat, ginger, garlic and lemongrass into the wok and fry briefly.

4. Add the bean sprouts and fry briefly then stir in the chicken broth (stock). Add the coconut milk and 1 tablespoon curry paste and bring to a boil.

5. Draw the wok away from the heat and season with lime juice and fish sauce. Remove the lemongrass.

6. Ladle the soup into bowls and serve garnished with mint leaves.

SWEETCORN AND CRAB MEAT SOUP

Ingredients

1 egg white

1 tsp sesame oil

4 cups / 1 liter chicken broth (stock)

2 cups / 400 g drained canned or thawed frozen corn

1 tbsp rice wine or dry sherry

1 tbsp light soy sauce

2 inch / 5 cm piece fresh ginger root, peeled and grated

1 tsp sugar

Salt and freshly ground pepper, to taste

2 tsp cornstarch (cornflour), mixed to a smooth paste in 1 tbsp water

1½ cups / 250 g flaked crabmeat, picked over to remove shells

To garnish:

2 scallions (spring onions), thinly sliced

1 tbsp chopped cilantro (fresh coriander) leaves

Method
Prep and cook time: 30 min

1. In a small bowl, whisk together the egg white and sesame oil; set aside.

2. Bring the broth (stock) to a boil in a large saucepan. Add the corn and simmer for around 4 minutes.

3. Add the rice wine or sherry, soy sauce, ginger, sugar, and a little salt and pepper; heat through.

4. Stir in the cornstarch (cornflour) mixture and bring to a boil, then add the crab.

5. Slowly add the egg white mixture, stirring constantly; heat through and season with salt and pepper. Serve garnished with scallions (spring onion) and cilantro (coriander).

POTATO CURRY SOUP WITH CHICKEN

Ingredients

2–3 large boiling potatoes

2 large carrots

1 onion

2 chicken breasts

2 tbsp oil

1 tbsp curry powder

½ tsp cinnamon

2 tsp garam masala

2½ cups / 600 ml vegetable broth (stock)

1¼ cups / 300 g yogurt

3 tbsp chopped mint leaves

Salt & freshly milled pepper

Method

Prep and cook time: 35 min

1. Peel the potatoes, then rinse and dice. Peel the carrots, cut in half lengthways, then cut diagonally. Peel the onion and cut into slices.

2. Cut the chicken into bite-size pieces and fry in hot oil. Season to taste with salt, pepper and curry powder. Take out of the skillet.

3. Sauté the potatoes, carrots and onions in the meat fat, stirring continually. Season to taste with salt and pepper. Stir in the rest of the spices and pour in the vegetable broth (stock). Simmer gently for about 10 minutes. Add the chicken pieces and simmer for a further 4–5 minutes. Season to taste.

4. Mix the yogurt with 2 tablespoons of chopped mint.

5. Pour the soup into serving bowls and garnish with a spoonful of yogurt sauce and some chopped mint.

RED LENTIL SOUP

Ingredients

4 tbsp clarified butter or oil

1 onion, finely sliced

2 garlic cloves

Thumb-size piece ginger, peeled and chopped

1 red chili pepper, deseeded and finely chopped

2 tsp curry powder

1 tsp curcuma (turmeric)

1½ cups / 300 g red lentils

1 cup / 200 g canned tomatoes, chopped

3 cups / 750 ml chicken broth (stock)

Salt and pepper

2 scallions (spring onions), sliced diagonally, to garnish

2 tbsp chopped cilantro (fresh coriander), to garnish

Method

Prep and cook time: 25 min

1. Heat the butter in a deep pan and fry the onions until soft but not brown.

2. Add the garlic, ginger, chili pepper, curry powder and curcuma (turmeric) and cook for 2 minutes then add the lentils and stir well.

3. Add the tomatoes and chicken broth (stock), season with salt and pepper and simmer very gently for about 20 minutes or until the lentils are tender.

4. Serve garnished with scallions (spring onions) and cilantro (fresh coriander).

BOUILLON NIPPON WITH DUCK BREAST

Ingredients

1 duck breast fillet
(about 10 oz / 300 g)

Salt & freshly milled pepper

1 inch / 3 cm piece fresh ginger

1 chili

6 cups / 1½ liters strong chicken
broth (stock)

1 large carrot

2 scallions (spring onions)

2 oz / 50 g narrow ribbon noodles

2 oz / 60 g small bean sprouts
(soybean or mung bean)

3½ oz / 100 g slice tofu

1 hard-boiled egg

Soy sauce

Method

Prep and cook time: 1 hour

1. Score the skin of the duck breast in a diamond pattern and season with salt and pepper. Then lay in a cold skillet, skin side down, and heat. Turn over as soon as the fat runs. Fry for about 7 minutes, then turn and fry for about a further 7 minutes until crisp. Take out and set aside.

2. Peel and slice the ginger. Wash and deseed the chili. Put the ginger and chili into the broth (stock), cover and simmer for 15 minutes. Strain the broth through a sieve.

3. Peel the carrot and cut into thin strips lengthways (or into shapes using a cutter). Wash and trim the scallions (spring onions) and cut into rings at an angle.

4. Cook the noodles according to the package instructions, drain and refresh in cold water.

5. Rinse the bean sprouts in cold water and drain. Dice the tofu. Shell and slice the egg. Cut the duck breast into thin slices.

6. Divide the noodles, vegetables, tofu, egg and meat between soup bowls, add hot broth and season to taste with soy sauce. Serve at once.

THAI TOM YUM SOUP

Ingredients

2 chicken legs

2 red chili peppers

10 oz / 300 g string beans

4 cups / 1 liter beef broth (stock)

2 kaffir lime leaves

1 stalk lemongrass, slightly crushed

1 tsp freshly grated ginger

1 tsp tamarind concentrate

10 oz / 300 g mini corns

Fish sauce

Chili sauce

Soybean sprouts, to garnish

Method

Prep and cook time: 25 min

1. Remove the skin from the chicken, remove the bone and cut into bite-size pieces.

2. Wash the chili peppers and cut into rings. Wash and trim the string beans.

3. Bring the beef broth (stock), kaffir lime leaves, lemongrass, ginger and tamarind concentrate to a boil. Add the string beans and simmer gently for about 2–3 minutes. Add the chicken, chili and mini corns and simmer for another 5–6 minutes.

4. Season with fish sauce and chili sauce. Remove the lemongrass stick, garnish with the soybean sprouts and serve.

CHICKEN SOUP WITH ALMONDS

Ingredients

4 tbsp sunflower oil

4 chicken breasts, skinned and
 cut into chunks

2 onions, finely chopped

3 garlic cloves, chopped

2 tsp ground cumin

½ tsp cayenne pepper

1 tsp each of: ground ginger, ground
coriander and curcuma (turmeric)

$^2/_3$ cup / 100 g ground almonds

2 cups / 500 ml chicken broth (stock)

Salt and pepper

½ cup / 125 ml yogurt

1 cup / 75 g flaked almonds

1 tsp saffron threads, to garnish

2 tbsp sesame seeds, lightly toasted
in a dry pan, to garnish

Method

Prep and cook time: 45 min

1. Heat the oil in a wide pan and fry the
chicken pieces for 5 minutes or until lightly
browned all over. Remove from the pan and
keep warm.

2. Gently fry the onions in the pan until
softened but not brown then stir in the garlic
and spices. Cook for 2 minutes, stirring all
the time.

3. Add the ground almonds and chicken
broth (stock), season with salt and pepper
then add the chicken and simmer very
gently for 20 minutes.

4. Spoon in the yogurt and flaked almonds
and simmer very gently for 5 more minutes.

5. Serve the soup in warmed bowls with
the saffron threads and sesame seeds
sprinkled over.

SHIITAKE MUSHROOM AND NOODLE SOUP

Ingredients

2 tbsp vegetable oil

1 cup / 125 g sliced shiitake mushrooms

4 scallions (spring onions), trimmed and chopped

1 clove garlic, minced

1 carrot, cut into very thin sticks

¾ cup / 75 g halved snow peas (mangetout)

5 cups / 1.25 liters chicken broth (stock)

2 tbsp light soy sauce

2 tbsp dry sherry

2 oz / 50 g instant or thin rice noodles (vermicelli)

1 cup / 200 g baby corn

Method

Prep and cook time: 20 min

1. Heat the oil in a skillet or wok, then add the mushrooms and stir-fry for 2 minutes.

2. Add the scallions (spring onions), garlic, carrot and snow peas (mangetout) and stir-fry for a further 2 minutes. Pour in the broth (stock), soy sauce and sherry and bring to a boil.

3. Add the rice noodles and baby corn and cook for 3 minutes or until noodles and corn are tender. Serve in bowls.

SALMON CURRY SOUP

Ingredients

3 tbsp ghee or clarified butter

1 onion, finely chopped

1 tbsp curry powder

1 tsp curcuma (turmeric)

½ small fresh pineapple, cut into small chunks

1 small apple, peeled and chopped into small pieces

1 banana, sliced

4 tbsp coconut milk

2 cups /450 ml chicken broth (stock)

1 cup / 225 ml milk

Salt and pepper

1 lb / 450 g asparagus spears

12 oz / 350 g salmon fillet

1 tsp lemon juice

Chopped fresh parsley, to garnish

1 red chili, deseeded and cut into rings, to garnish

Method

Prep and cook time: 40 min

1. Heat 1 tbsp of the ghee in a saucepan. Add the onion and fry until softened but not browned. Sprinkle the curry powder and curcuma (turmeric) over the onion and cook for 1 minute.

3 Add the fruit to the onion and heat quickly. Pour in the coconut milk, broth (stock) and milk and bring to the boil.

4 Remove from the heat and, using a hand-held blender, blend to form a purée. Season to taste with salt and pepper.

5 Cut the asparagus spears into small lengths and cook in a saucepan of boiling salted water for about 5 minutes, until tender but still firm to the bite. Drain and set aside.

6 Cut the salmon into bite-sized pieces, drizzle over the lemon juice and season with salt.

7 Heat the remaining 2 tbsp ghee or clarified butter in a non-stick skillet (frying pan). Add the salmon and quickly fry on both sides over a very high heat. Remove from the pan and keep warm. Quickly fry the asparagus in the same pan.

8 Serve the hot soup in small bowls, add the salmon and the asparagus and sprinkle the chili rings over the top. Garnish with parsley.

MISO SOUP WITH VEGETABLES

Ingredients

2 tbsp miso

1 tbsp vegetable broth granules

1 small carrot, peeled and cut into matchsticks

¼ nori sheet, cut into thin strips

1 bunch radishes, trimmed and halved

½ tsp ground ginger

Salt

Method

Prep and cook time: 15 min

1. Put the miso into a pan with 3 tbsp water and heat until it dissolves. Add 4 cups / 1 liter water and the broth granules.

2. Add the radishes, carrots and ginger to the soup and simmer for about 4 minutes. Season to taste with salt. Divide the nori strips between 4 bowls, ladle the hot soup over them and serve.

CURRIED PARSNIP SOUP

Ingredients

Serves 6

2 tbsp / 25 g butter

1 tbsp oil

1 onion, finely chopped

1lb / 450 g parsnips, diced

1 tsp ground cumin

1 tsp curry powder

4 cups / 1 liter vegetable broth (stock)

Salt and pepper

1$^{1}/_{3}$ cups / 300 ml milk

To garnish:

4 tbsp whipping cream

Chopped parsley

Method

Prep and cook time: 1 hour

1. Heat the butter and oil in a skillet (frying pan) and cook the onion for about 5 minutes until soft but not browned.

2. Add the parsnips and spices and cook for 2 minutes.

3. Pour in the broth (stock) and bring to a boil. Season to taste with salt and pepper. Cover and cook on a low heat for 45 minutes, until the parsnips are tender.

4. Purée the mixture in batches in a food processor or blender until smooth.

5. Stir in the milk, return to the pan and cook for a few minutes until hot.

6. Ladle into soup bowls, top with a swirl of cream and sprinkle with chopped parsley.

TAMARIND AND COCONUT SOUP

Ingredients

¹/₃ cup / 80 ml sesame oil

1 red onion, peeled and chopped

2 cloves garlic, peeled and chopped

1 red chili, chopped

1–2 tsp cumin

1 tsp ground coriander

2 very ripe plantains, peeled and cut into ½ inch (1 cm) slices

2½ cups / 600 ml chicken broth (stock)

¼ cup / 50 ml tamarind paste

1¼ cups / 300 ml unsweetened coconut milk

1 tsp sea salt

½ cup roughly chopped cilantro (coriander) leaves

½ cup roughly chopped fresh mint leaves

Method

Prep and cook time: 35 min

1. Heat the sesame oil in a large pan and add the red onion, garlic, half of the chili, cumin and ground coriander. Sauté for 5 minutes, stirring continuously so it doesn't stick.

2. Add the plantains, broth (stock), tamarind paste and coconut milk and bring to a boil. Turn the heat to a gentle simmer and cook until the plantains are soft, then remove from the heat.

3. Add the salt and purée the soup. Return to the heat and add the rest of the chili.

4. Stir in the cilantro (coriander) and mint just before serving.

CHICKEN NOODLE SOUP

Ingredients

10 oz / 300 g chicken breast, cut into bite-size pieces

1 tbsp cornstarch (cornflour)

2 tbsp sesame oil

1 garlic clove, finely chopped

½ inch / 1 cm piece ginger, peeled and finely chopped

1 tsp curcuma (turmeric)

4 cups / 1 liter vegetable broth (stock)

1 stick lemongrass, cut into strips

7 oz / 200 g rice noodles

1 small Napa cabbage (Chinese leaves), chopped

4 scallions (spring onions), chopped

8 cherry tomatoes, quartered

2 tomatoes, diced

4 tbsp light soy sauce

4 tbsp lime juice

Thai basil, to garnish

Method

Prep and cook time: 25 min

1 Mix the chicken pieces and the cornstarch (cornflour) in a bowl.

2 Heat the sesame oil in a saucepan and fry the chicken until lightly browned. Add the garlic, ginger, and curcuma (turmeric) and sauté, then pour in the vegetable broth (stock) and bring to a boil.

3 Add the lemongrass to the soup and simmer for about 5 minutes.

4 Put the rice noodles in the soup and simmer for a further 1–2 minutes over a low heat. Add the Napa cabbage (Chinese leaves), scallions (spring onions), cherry tomatoes, and tomatoes and warm thoroughly.

5 Season to taste with soy sauce and lime juice. Garnish with Thai basil and serve.

SCALLOP SOUP WITH CHILI AND LEMONGRASS

Ingredients

1 stick lemongrass

½ red chili

1 inch / 3 cm piece ginger, freshly grated

4 cups / 1 liter fish broth (stock)

1½ tbsp fish sauce

Salt & freshly milled pepper

1 tbsp lime juice

1 tbsp oil

4 scallops, ready prepared

Basil leaves, to garnish

Cilantro (coriander) leaves, to garnish

Method

Prep and cook time: 25 min

1. Remove the outer leaves from the lemongrass and finely chop. Wash the chili, remove the seeds and cut into rings. Peel the ginger and grate very finely.

2. Bring the fish broth (stock), fish sauce, lemongrass, ginger and chili to a boil and simmer for about 10 minutes. Season to taste with salt, pepper and lime juice.

3. In the meantime, heat the oil in a skillet and fry the scallops for about 1 minute on each side.

4. Put in the hot soup and leave to stand for a while. Season again, then spoon into bowls, garnish with the cilantro (coriander) and basil leaves and serve.

HOT AND SOUR SHRIMP SOUP

Ingredients

7 oz / 200 g straw mushrooms, enoki or white mushrooms

2 chilies

1 stalk lemongrass

4 cups / 1 liter chicken broth (stock)

12 whole shrimp (or prawns)

6 kaffir lime leaves

Juice of 1 lime

1 tsp galangal, freshly grated

Fish sauce

Cilantro (coriander) leaves to garnish

Method

Prep and cook time: 20 min

1. Clean the mushrooms. Slice the chilies. Shred the lemongrass very finely.

2. Put the chicken broth (stock) into a pan and bring to a boil. Put all the ingredients into the broth and cook very gently for 6–8 minutes. Add fish sauce to taste and serve scattered with cilantro (coriander).

PUMPKIN SOUP WITH CHICKEN

Ingredients

2 chicken breasts

1–2 tbsp light soy sauce

1 small pumpkin

1 onion

¾ inch / 2 cm piece of fresh ginger

2 tbsp dried jelly ear fungus

2 cups / 500 ml vegetable broth (stock)

1 red chili

1¾ cups / 400 ml coconut milk

2 or 3 tomatoes

Salt & freshly milled pepper

Thai basil, to garnish

Method

Prep and cook time: 45 min

1. Cut the chicken into strips and marinate in 1–2 tablespoons soy sauce. Peel, deseed and dice the pumpkin. Peel and slice the onion. Peel and finely chop the ginger. Chop the jelly ear fungus and soak in a little hot water.

2. Put the onion, ginger and pumpkin into a pan with the vegetable broth (stock). Slit the chili open lengthways, deseed and add to the pan. Cook for about 20 minutes with a lid on the pan. Then remove the chili and take half of the vegetables out of the broth (stock).

3. Finely purée the rest of the vegetables with the broth. Drain the jelly ear fungus and add to the soup with the coconut milk. Bring to a boil. Boil for 2–3 minutes, then return the vegetables to the soup.

4. Deseed the tomatoes and cut into pieces. Add to the soup with the chicken. Briefly bring to a boil, then cook gently for 7 minutes.

5. Season to taste and ladle into bowls. Serve garnished with basil.

SPICY BEEF SOUP

Ingredients

3½ oz / 100 g ribbon pasta

10 oz / 300 g beef

2 carrots

2 chili peppers

2 red bell peppers

7 oz / 200 g string beans

1 bunch scallions (spring onions)

3¼ cups / 800 ml beef broth (stock)

1 stick lemongrass, slightly crushed

2 kaffir lime leaves

Hot chili sauce

Fish sauce

Method
Prep and cook time: 35 min

1. Cook the pasta in boiling, salted water according to instructions on the packet until al dente. Rinse under cold water, then drain.

2. Cut the beef into thin strips. Peel the carrots and cut into strips. Finely chop the chili peppers, removing the seeds. Cut the bell peppers in half, remove the seeds and cut into strips. Wash the string beans and chop diagonally. Wash the scallions (spring onions) and cut diagonally into rings.

3. Bring the beef broth (stock), lemongrass and kaffir lime leaves to a boil. Add the beans, chili peppers and the carrots and simmer for about 5 minutes. Now add the scallions and the bell pepper and simmer for a further 5 minutes. Add the pasta and the beef for the last 4–5 minutes. Season with chili sauce and fish sauce. Remove the lemongrass and the lime leaves and serve.

CHICKEN LAKSA

Ingredients

For the paste:

2 garlic cloves, peeled

2 tbsp freshly chopped cilantro (coriander)

4 green chili peppers

1 large chopped onion

1 tsp shrimp paste

2 tsp oil

4 chicken breasts, skinned

4 oz / 100 g thin rice noodles

2 tbsp sesame oil

2 tbsp coconut cream

8 tbsp coconut milk

3¼ cups / 800 ml chicken broth (stock)

Juice of 2 limes

2 tbsp soy sauce

1 large handful bean sprouts

1 large handful choi sum or spinach

4 scallions (spring onions), trimmed and cut into strips

2 limes, cut into wedges

Cilantro (coriander) leaves, to garnish

Method

Prep and cook time: 25 min plus
24 hours marinating time

1. Purée the peeled garlic, chopped cilantro (coriander), chili peppers (minus seeds), onion, oil and shrimp paste.

2. Spread the chicken breasts with about half the paste and marinate in the refrigerator, covered, for about 24 hours.

3. Cut up the noodles with scissors and soak in hot water.

4. Then heat the sesame oil in a frying pan and brown the chicken breasts on both sides. Add the rest of the paste, the coconut cream and milk, the broth (stock), lime juice and soy sauce and simmer for about 8–10 minutes. Add the noodles, bean sprouts and choi sum (or spinach) and cook for about 1 minute to heat through.

5. Divide the noodles between 4 bowls, add a little of the sauce and vegetables to each. Then place a chicken breast and the rest of the vegetables on top of each bowl of noodles. Garnish with scallions (spring onions), lime wedges and cilantro (coriander) leaves.

STARTERS
AND
SALADS

NAAN BREAD WITH MANGO CHUTNEY

Ingredients

⅓ cup / 75 ml milk	3 oz / 75 g plain yogurt	2 tbsp brown sugar
⅓ oz / 10 g yeast, fresh	1 small egg	1–2 tbsp red wine vinegar
2 tsp sugar	Oil, for the cookie sheet	Salt & freshly milled pepper
2½ cups / 250 g all-purpose (plain) flour	1 bunch parsley, chopped	1 stick cinnamon
½ tsp salt	For the mango chutney:	2 cloves
½ tsp baking powder	7oz / 200 g mango, peeled and diced	1 bay leaf
1 tbsp oil	2 tbsp golden raisins (sultanas)	1 tbsp paprika

Method

Prep and cook time: Bread: 30 min plus 1 hour 15 mins rising time
Chutney: 30 min plus cooling time

1. Warm the milk and pour in a bowl. Crumble the yeast over the top and add 1 tsp sugar. Stir until dissolved and leave for 15 minutes until frothy.

2. Sift the flour into a large bowl, add the salt and the baking powder and mix. Now add 1 teaspoon sugar, the milk and yeast mixture, the oil, the yogurt and the egg and knead to form a smooth dough. Form a ball, cover and leave in a warm place for about an hour to rise.

3. Oil the cookie sheet and pre-heat the oven to 475°F (230°C / Gas Mark 8).

4. Knead the dough again, together with the chopped parsley and divide into 4 pieces.

Make 4 balls, then roll out on a floured surface to a naan form. Place on the cookie sheet and bake in the oven for about 8 minutes until golden brown.

5. To make the mango chutney mix all ingredients together with 3–4 tablespoons water. Bring to a boil, stirring continually, Simmer for 10–15 minutes until the mango is soft. Season to taste, then let cool. Remove the bay leaf, cloves and cinnamon stick.

6. Pour into small bowls and serve together with the fresh naan bread.

LAMB SAMOSAS

Ingredients

For the dough:

3 cups / 300 g all-purpose (plain) flour

4 tbsp clarified butter

1 tsp salt

For the filling:

4 tbsp clarified butter

½ tsp ground ginger

½ tsp ground cumin

½ tsp ground coriander

½ tsp chili powder

1 tsp garam masala

1 onion, very finely chopped

1 lb / 450 g ground (minced) lamb

1¼ cups / 125 g frozen peas, thawed

1 tsp salt

Approx 2 pints / 1 liter vegetable oil, for frying

Method

Prep and cook time: 1 hour

1. For the dough, mix the flour, clarified butter and salt together with enough warm water to form a soft dough. Turn onto a floured board and knead for 3 minutes then return to the bowl and let rest while you make the filling.

2. For the filling, heat the clarified butter in a wide pan and gently fry the spices for 2 minutes.

3. Add the onion, cook until softened then stir in the lamb, peas and salt. Cook for about 5 minutes or until the meat is well browned then set aside.

4. Divide the dough into 8 pieces and roll each one out on a floured board to make a circle about 8 inches / 20 cm in diameter.

5. Cut each circle in half, place a little of the filling on one half of each semi-circle, moisten the edges with water then fold over the pastry and press together the edges to make a tight seal.

6. Heat the oil in a deep pan until small bubble rise to the surface then deep fry the samosas in batches for 3–4 minutes, turning once, until they are golden brown.

7. Drain the samosas on kitchen paper and serve warm.

Makes 16

VEGETABLE SAMOSAS

Ingredients

For the filling:

1 onion, finely chopped

1 cup / 300 g cauliflower florets

1 cup / 100 g frozen green beans, chopped into small pieces

2–3 tbsp ghee or clarified butter

½ tsp cumin seeds

2 tsp freshly grated ginger

½ tsp chili powder

Spices mix: 1 tsp each of coriander, sweet paprika and garam masala

1 cup / 125 g frozen peas

Salt

For the pastry:

3 cups / 300 g all-purpose (plain) flour

4 tbsp ghee or clarified butter

1 tsp salt

Oil for deep frying, plus some for the work surface

Method

Prep and cook time: 1 hour

1. For the pastry, put the flour, ghee or clarified butter, salt and ¾ cup (175 ml) water in a bowl. Mix the ingredients together and knead to a smooth dough. Cover and leave to rest for about 20 minutes.

2. Blanch the cauliflower florets and the beans in boiling, salted water for 4 minutes, then place in cold water and drain.

3. Heat the ghee in a saucepan. Fry the cumin over a medium heat for about 1 minute then add the ginger and all the other spices, apart from the salt, and stir. Add the onions and sauté, then add all the vegetables and fry for about 3 minutes, stirring occasionally. Reduce the heat, cover with a lid and simmer for about 5 minutes in the juices. Season with salt and let cool.

4. Divide the dough into 8 portions. Oil a large, wooden board and roll out each ball to a rectangle 8 x 4 inches (20 x 10 cm) in size. Now cut in half to form 2 squares.

5. Divide the filling between the pastry wrappers and fold each wrapper diagonally in half to form a triangle. Press the edges down firmly.

6. Heat the oil in a large saucepan over a medium heat. Fry the samosas in the hot oil for 3–4 minutes, a few at a time. Turn once. Place the cooked samosas on paper towels to drain. Keep warm until ready to serve.

SPRING ROLLS WITH CHILI DIP

Ingredients

For the filling:

3½ cups / 100 g glass noodles

8 oz / 250 g carrots

8 oz / 250 g white cabbage

1½ cups / 200 g soybean sprouts

3 cloves garlic

4 cups / 1 liter oil, to fry

7 oz / 200 g ground (minced) beef or finely chopped shrimp (prawns)

Salt & freshly milled pepper

2 tsp sugar

1 egg

About 40 spring roll wrappers

1 jar Thai sweet chili dip, to serve

Method
Prep and cook time: 50 min

1. Soak the glass noodles in cold water for 30 minutes.

2. Peel and roughly grate the carrots. Shred the cabbage finely. Rinse the soybean sprouts and drain well. Put all these ingredients into a bowl and mix.

3. Peel and finely chop the garlic. Heat 3 tbsp of the oil in a skillet or wok and briefly fry the garlic. Add the ground meat and fry for 3–5 minutes, breaking it up until brown all over. Season with salt and pepper and leave to cool slightly.

4. Drain the glass noodles, cut into about 2 inch (4 cm) lengths and add to the vegetables. Season with salt, pepper and a little sugar. Add the cooled ground meat and mix well.

5. Lightly beat the egg. Take 1 spring roll wrapper and place on a work surface. Put about 2 heaped tablespoons of the filling across the middle of the wrapper. Turn in the sides and roll up to make a roll about 4 inches (10 cm) long. Use a little beaten egg to stick the edge of the spring roll. Repeat with the other wrappers.

6. Heat the remaining oil in a wok or skillet. (The oil is hot enough when bubbles form on the handle of a wooden spoon held in the oil.) Fry the spring rolls in batches for about 6–8 minutes until golden brown. Take out, drain on a paper towel and serve with chili dip.

CHICKPEA FRITTERS

Ingredients

1 stale bread roll, soaked in water

2 cups / 400 g canned chickpeas, rinsed and drained

1 onion, peeled and finely chopped

1 garlic clove, peeled and finely chopped

2 tbsp freshly chopped cilantro (fresh coriander)

½ tsp ground coriander

½ tsp ground cumin

¼ tsp baking powder

1 egg

Bread crumbs

Vegetable oil, for frying

Salt and freshly ground pepper

Method

Prep and cook time: 30 min

1. Squeeze the bread roll well to remove excess liquid.

2. Purée the chickpeas with the bread roll, onions and garlic in a processor.

3. Mix in the cilantro (coriander leaves), ground coriander, cumin, baking powder and egg, adding breadcrumbs if the dough is too moist. Season with salt and pepper.

4. Heat the oil in a skillet and drop in spoonfuls of the mixture, flattening slightly. Fry on each side for 2–3 minutes until golden brown.

SHRIMP BALLS

Ingredients

2 scallions (spring onions), only the white parts

1 lb 6 oz / 600 g peeled shrimp (or prawns), pre-prepared

1 tsp ginger, grated

2 garlic cloves, finely chopped

1 egg white

1 tbsp cornstarch (cornflour)

Salt

Cayenne pepper

Soy sauce

1 pak choi

Method

Prep and cook time: 30 min

1. Trim the scallions (spring onions), halve lengthwise and chop very finely.

2. Purée half of the the shrimps (or prawns) very finely. Finely chop the other half. Combine with the scallions, ginger, garlic and the egg white. If the mixture is too soft, work in some cornstarch (cornflour). Season with salt, a little soy sauce and cayenne pepper and form into about 20 balls with moist hands.

3. Arrange the pak choi loosely on a base of the bamboo steamer. Drizzle with soy sauce. Place the shrimp balls on top and steam over boiling water with the lid on for about 10 minutes.

4. If you wish, serve with chili or soy sauce dip.

POTATO PAKORAS WITH YOGURT SAUCE

Ingredients

1 lb / 450 g potatoes

1 cup / 75 g gram (chickpea) flour

$^1/_3$ cup / 50 g cornmeal (polenta)

1 tsp fennel seeds

3 green chili peppers, deseeded and finely chopped

2 tbsp chopped cilantro (fresh coriander) leaves

1 onion, finely chopped

Sunflower oil, for frying

For the yogurt sauce:

1 cup / 250 ml yogurt

1 tsp sugar

1 pinch salt

1 tbsp chopped cilantro (fresh coriander) leaves

1 tbsp chopped mint leaves

Salt and pepper

Method

Prep and cook time: 1 hour 30 min

1. Cook the potatoes in salted water for 30 minutes or until soft and then mash.

2. Mix the gram flour, cornmeal (polenta) and fennel seeds in a bowl. Stir in the chili, cilantro (fresh coriander) and onion. Then add the potatoes and as much water as necessary to form a thick, kneadable dough.

3. Heat the oil in a deep skillet until bubbles appear on a wooden spoon held in the fat.

4. Drop tsp-sized portions of the dough into the oil and fry until golden yellow. Remove from the pan and pat dry on kitchen paper.

5. To make the yogurt sauce, mix all the ingredients together and season to taste. Serve the potato pakoras with the yogurt sauce.

SPRING ROLL WITH CHILI-NUT DIP

Ingredients

For the dip:

1/3 cup / 50 g peanuts

4 tbsp sweet chili sauce

2 tbsp fish sauce

1 tbsp chopped cilantro (coriander) leaves

For the spring rolls:

4 sheets rice paper

2 carrots

14 oz / 400 g can crab meat

1 bunch Thai basil

Method
Prep and cook time: 30 min

1. To make the dip, roughly chop the peanuts and toast in a dry skillet until golden brown.

2. Pour in the chili sauce and fish sauce and stir. Add a little water if necessary. Remove from the heat and let cool. Add the chopped cilantro (coriander).

3. For the spring rolls, soak the rice paper according to instructions on the packet.

4. Peel the carrots and cut into thin strips. Drain the crab meat well. Pick the Thai basil leaves from their stem.

5. Place some of the carrots, crab meat and Thai basil leaves in the center of each rice paper and roll. Cut each in half and serve with the dip.

STUFFED BANANA LEAVES

Ingredients

1 lb 12 oz / 800 g tofu

Soy sauce

1 lb 2 oz / 500 g mixed ground (minced) beef and pork

1 chili, finely chopped

1 tsp grated ginger

1 garlic clove, finely chopped

6 banana leaves, each about 6 x 2 inches / 15 x 5 cm

Toothpicks (cocktail sticks)

Method

Prep and cook time: 25 min plus 30 min marinating time

1. Cut the tofu into 24 cubes and marinate in plenty of soy sauce for about 30 minutes.

2. Mix the ground meat with the chili, ginger and garlic. Season with a little soy sauce and form into 12 balls.

3. Place a meatball in the center of each banana leaf, put a cube of tofu on either side and wrap the banana leaf around them. Secure with toothpicks (cocktail sticks) and cook on all sides on a broiler (grill), or in the oven at 350°F (180°C / Gas Mark 4) for about 8 minutes.

SEAFOOD TEMPURA

Ingredients

3 cups / 750 ml sunflower oil

1 cup / 100 g all purpose (plain) flour

1 tsp baking powder

½ tsp salt

1 egg yolk

½ cup /125 ml chilled sparkling mineral water

2 lbs / 800 g mixed prepared seafood, shrimps, squid, whitebait, sole fillets

Method

Prep and cook time: 20 min

1. Beat together the flour, baking powder, salt and egg yolk with enough water to make a batter.

2. Heat the oil in a wok or deep skillet until smoking.

3. Cook the seafood in batches, dipping pieces into the batter then deep frying them into the oil until they are golden brown and crisp.

4. Drain on kitchen paper and serve immediately.

THAI FISH AND SHRIMP ROLLS

Ingredients

10 oz / 300 g fish fillet

5 oz / 150 g peeled shrimp (or prawns)

3 small green chilies

2/3 cup / 50 g coconut flakes

1 tsp shrimp paste

Salt

Freshly ground pepper

1 tsp cane sugar

12 skewers or 6 lemongrass stalks, halved lengthways

Oil, for frying

For the chili sauce:

1 lb 10 oz / 750 g fully ripe tomatoes

3 red chilies

1 onion

2 tbsp olive oil

2 garlic cloves

1 tbsp tomato paste

1 tbsp vinegar

2½ tbsp sugar

Salt & freshly ground pepper

1 tsp cornflour

Method

Prep and cook time: 1 hour

1. Cut the fish fillet and the shrimp (or prawns) into pieces and mash finely in a blender.

2. Core and finely chop the chili, grind in a mortar with the coconut flakes, shrimp paste, a little salt, pepper and sugar. Then mix smoothly with the ground fish and shrimp mixture.

3. Form the mixture into a thick roll, cut the roll into about 12 equal sized disks and shape the disks into rectangles (about 1 x 3 inches / 3 x 8 cm). Wrap each skewer or lemongrass stalk with a rectangle and roll the dough into a smooth shape around the skewers on a work surface, using lightly oiled hands.

4. Pour oil into a deep pan to a depth of about ½ inch (1 cm) and heat. Fry the skewers in batches over medium heat for about 7 minutes until crispy on all sides. Serve with sweet and sour chili sauce.

5. For the sauce, scald the tomatoes for a few seconds, peel, quarter, core and chop. Finely chop the chilies, removing the seeds and white parts.

6. Peel and chop the onion, sweat in hot oil in a pan together with the chilies. Crush the garlic, add to the pan, mix the tomato paste and the tomatoes as well and leave to sweat for a few minutes. Add the sugar, vinegar, salt and 1 bowl of water, cover with a lid and let simmer for 15 minutes.

7. Mix the cornstarch (cornflour) with 1 tbsp cold water evenly, stir this mixture into the sauce, bring to a boil and let thicken a little bit. Season with salt and pepper.

VEGETABLE TEMPURA

Ingredients

3 cups / 750 g sunflower oil

1 cup / 100 g all-purpose (plain) flour

1 tsp baking powder

1 egg white, lightly whisked

½ cup / 125 ml chilled sparkling mineral water

1 eggplant, sliced lengthways

1 carrot, sliced lengthways

1 bunch asparagus, trimmed

1 red bell pepper, deseeded and sliced

1 zucchini (courgette), sliced lengthways

2 cups / 350 g broccoli florets

Method

Prep and cook time: 20 min

1. Sift the flour and baking powder into a bowl and fold in the egg white. Add enough water to make a thin batter.

2. Heat the oil in a wok or deep skillet until smoking.

3. Coat the vegetables in batter and deep fry them in the oil in batches until crisp.

4. Drain on kitchen paper and serve immediately.

THAI SAGO BALL WITH PEANUT FILLING

Ingredients

14 oz / 400 g sago

7 oz / 200 g can of corn

2/3 cup / 100 g peanuts

3 garlic cloves

1 onion

3 tbsp oil

1 tsp freshly grated ginger

2 tbsp chopped cilantro (coriander) leaves

2 tbsp soy sauce

Fish sauce

Cayenne pepper

Method

Prep and cook time: 40 min

1. Wash the sago in a sieve with plenty of cold water, then put in a bowl. Pour ½ cup (120 ml) of water into the bowl and knead the sago to a smooth dough. Let rest uncovered.

2. For the filling wash the corn and let drain. Chop the peanuts. Peel and finely chop the garlic. Likewise, peel and finely chop the onion.

3. Gently fry the garlic in hot oil until golden brown and take half of it out of the pan for the garnish.

4. Add the onion to the garlic remaining in the pan, fry until golden brown, then add the ginger, peanuts and corn. Remove from the heat, work in the cilantro (coriander) and soy sauce and season well with fish sauce.

5. Form walnut-sized balls from the sago dough, flatten the balls, fill each one with 1–2 teaspoons. of the mixture and roll the dough back into a ball.

6. Steam for about 15 minutes in a bamboo steamer. Serve garnished with the rest of the garlic.

ONION BHAJIS WITH MANGO CHUTNEY

Ingredients

For the bhajis:

1 tbsp coriander seeds

1 tbsp cumin seeds

1 cup / 75 g gram flour

½ tsp baking powder

1 tsp salt

2 onions, grated

Oil, for frying

For the chutney:

2 tsp coriander seeds

2 tsp cumin seeds

1 tsp black onion seeds

1 cup / 250 ml white wine vinegar

1 cup / 250 g muscovado sugar

1 tsp salt

½ red chili pepper, deseeded and finely chopped

2 mangoes, peeled, stoned removed and cut into chunks

Method

Prep and cook time: 1 hour

1. For the chutney, lightly toast the coriander seeds, cumin seeds and black onion seeds in a hot, dry pan for 30 seconds.

2. Put the vinegar and sugar in a small pan and heat until the sugar has dissolved then add the toasted seeds, the salt and chili and let bubble for 5 minutes then add the mangoes and cook very gently for 20 minutes, stirring from time to time, or until very thick, then set aside.

3. For the bhajis, lightly toast the coriander seeds and cumin seeds in a hot, dry pan.

4. Sift the flour into a bowl and add the toasted seeds, baking powder, salt and grated onions. Add just enough water to make a very thick batter.

5. Heat the oil in a deep pan until bubbles appear on a wooden spoon held in the oil. Drop small balls of the batter into the oil in batches and deep fry for 3–4 minutes or until golden brown. Drain on kitchen paper and serve with the mango chutney.

DEEP-FRIED CORN FRITTERS

Ingredients

14 oz / 400 g can corn kernels

5 oz / 150 g ground (minced) pork

2 cloves garlic, peeled

1 tbsp sugar

2 eggs

About 1 tbsp cornstarch (cornflour)

Fish sauce

Cayenne pepper

Oil for deep-frying

Toothpicks (cocktail sticks)

Method

Prep and cook time: 20 min

1. Drain the corn kernels well. Finely purée half of the corn with the ground pork, garlic, sugar, eggs and 1 tablespoon cornstarch (cornflour).

2. Then mix in the rest of the corn kernels and add a little more cornstarch if necessary. Season with fish sauce and cayenne pepper.

3. With damp hands form the mixture into small balls. Heat the oil and fry for 2–3 minutes, turning occasionally, until golden brown.

4. Drain on paper towel and serve speared on toothpicks.

SHRIMP AND SCALLOP SKEWERS

Ingredients

4 large shrimp (or prawns), deveined and peeled

4 medium scallops

1 stalk lemongrass

4 tbsp olive oil

2 tbsp lemon juice

2 cloves garlic, minced

1 good pinch saffron threads, crumbled

Salt and freshly ground pepper

4 small red chilies

About 4 oz / 100 g cellophane noodles

2 tbsp vegetable oil

2 scallions (spring onions), thinly sliced on the diagonal

1–2 tbsp dry white wine

1 good pinch curcuma (turmeric)

1 head baby bok choy, quartered

Method

Prep and cook time: 40 min

1 Preheat the grill. Quarter the lemongrass stalk lengthwise and thread 1 shrimp (or prawn) and 1 scallop onto each piece.

2 In a small bowl, combine the olive oil, lemon juice, garlic and saffron threads; season with salt and pepper. Brush the lemongrass skewers and the chilies with the marinade and grill, turning and brushing frequently with the marinade, 3–4 minutes.

3 Meanwhile, cook the noodles according to the package instructions; drain and set aside.

4 Heat the oil in a skillet and add the scallions (spring onions); sauté briefly. Add the wine and turmeric; bring to a boil, scraping up browned bits from the skillet, and cook until the scallions are glazed. Set aside and season with salt and pepper.

5 Place a bok choy piece on each of 4 plates. Add the noodles and sprinkle with scallions. Place a shrimp and scallop skewer and a chili on top and serve.

CHICKPEA SALAD WITH SATAY CHICKEN SKEWERS

Ingredients

3 tbsp smooth peanut butter

½ cup / 125 ml olive oil

1 tbsp honey

Juice of 1 lime

2 chicken breasts, skinned and cut into strips

4 cups / 800 g canned chickpeas, drained and rinsed

2 red onion, finely chopped

2 red chilies, seeds removed and finely chopped

1 cup / 25 g chopped parsley

Juice of 1 lemon

Salt and freshly ground pepper

Method

Prep and cook time: 15 min plus 30 min to marinate

1. Blend the peanut butter with 2 tbsp of oil, the honey and the lime juice. Pour over the chicken strips, mix well and set aside for 30 minutes.

2. Mix the chickpeas with the chopped onion, chilies and parsley. Mix the remaining oil with the lemon juice, season with salt and pepper and pour over the chickpeas.

3. Remove the chicken strips from the marinade and thread onto wooden skewers.

4. Cook the chicken under a hot broiler (grill) for 5 minutes or until cooked through, turning once. Serve with the chickpea salad.

CHICKEN KEBABS WITH PEANUT SAUCE

Ingredients

½ cup / 125 ml sesame oil

1 garlic clove, chopped

2 red chilies, chopped

2 tbsp honey

1 cup / 250 ml smooth peanut butter

1 tbsp soy sauce

1 tsp fish sauce

Juice of 2 limes

2 chicken breasts, skinned and sliced

1 tbsp light oil

Chilies and lime wedges, to garnish

Method

Prep and cook time: 25 min

1. Heat the oil in a small pan and gently cook the garlic and chilies until soft. Stir in the honey, peanut butter, soy sauce, fish sauce and lime juice. Bring to a boil and simmer for 5 minutes.

2. Thread the chicken strips onto wooden skewers and brush with a little oil.

3. Heat a griddle pan and cook the chicken skewers until browned and cooked through.

4. Serve the chicken skewers drizzled with the sauce, garnish with whole chilies and lime wedges, and serve the remaining sauce alongside for dipping.

DICED SALMON WITH SOY DIP

Ingredients

1 lb 2 oz / 500 g salmon fillets, without skin, cut into bite-size cubes

For the marinade:

2 lemons, juice and zest

1 tbsp whole grain mustard

1 tbsp olive oil

For the dip:

1 red chili

1 scallion (spring onion)

5 tbsp light soy sauce

1 tbsp chopped cilantro (coriander) leaves

Salt and freshly ground pepper

Method

Prep and cook time: 20 min plus 30 min marinating time

1. Mix together all ingredients for the marinade and marinate the salmon cubes for about 30 minutes.

2. Remove the salmon from the marinade and place under a hot broiler (grill) for 2–3 minutes until lightly browned. Brush with marinade from time to time.

3. For the dip, de-seed and finely chop the chili. Trim the scallion (spring onion) and cut into rings.

4. Mix all the dip ingredients and season to taste. Serve the salmon with the dip.

SHRIMP AND TOMATO KEBABS WITH THAI SAUCE

Ingredients

6 tbsp soy sauce

2 tbsp fish sauce

3 tbsp sesame oil

Juice of 2 limes

2 tbsp honey

2 red chilies, seeds removed and finely chopped

2 garlic cloves, finely chopped

2 scallions (spring onions), finely chopped

1½ lb / 675 g large shrimps (prawns), tails and black veins removed

1 lb / 450 g cherry tomatoes, halved

Lime wedges, to garnish

Method

Prep and cook time: 20 min plus 30 min to marinate

1. Mix the soy sauce, fish sauce, 2 tbsp of sesame oil, the lime juice and honey in a large bowl.

2. Add the chopped chilies, garlic and scallions (spring onions) and mix in the shrimps (prawns). Set aside to marinate for 30 minutes, turning from time to time.

3. Heat the broiler (grill) to a medium setting.

4. Remove the shrimps from the marinade, brush the tomato halves with the remaining oil and thread onto wooden skewers alternating with the shrimps.

5. Heat the marinade in a small pan until reduced and slightly sticky. Set aside.

6. Cook the kebabs under the broiler, turning frequently, for about 6 minutes or until the shrimps are cooked through.

7. Serve the kebabs with the warm marinade drizzled over and lime wedges to garnish.

CHICKEN WINGS WITH SESAME SEEDS

Ingredients

3 tbsp olive oil

4 tbsp honey

2 tbsp Dijon mustard

Juice of 1 lemon

12 chicken wings

4 tbsp sesame seeds

Salt and freshly ground pepper

Method

Prep and cook time: 30 min plus
1 hour to marinate

1. Whisk together the oil, honey, mustard and lemon juice to make a marinade. Season with salt and pepper.

2. Put the chicken wings into a large bowl, pour over the marinade and mix well. Set aside for at least 1 hour, turning from time to time.

3. Heat the oven to 400F (200C / Gas Mark 6).

4. Toast the sesame seeds in a dry skillet until lightly browned. Set aside.

5. Remove the chicken wings from the marinade and put onto a cookie sheet. Roast in the oven for 15–20 minutes, turning once, until cooked through and browned all over.

6. Sprinkle the chicken wings with the toasted sesame seeds and serve warm or cold.

SWEET POTATO AND SHRIMP CAKES

Ingredients

8 oz / 225 g sweet potato

Salt and pepper

7 oz / 200 g canned chickpeas, drained

1 small onion

1 garlic clove

1 lb / 450 g peeled cooked shrimp (prawns)

2 tbsp chopped fresh cilantro (coriander)

2 tbsp olive oil

Few sprigs of mint, to garnish

Lime wedges, to serve

For the dip:

2 tbsp sweet chili sauce

1 tsp dark soy sauce

Method

Prep and cook time: 40 min

1. Put the unpeeled sweet potato in a saucepan of salted water, bring to the boil and cook for 10 minutes. Let cool, peel and grate coarsely.

2. Put the chickpeas in a food processor and blend until smooth or mash with a fork. Put in a bowl. Finely chop the onion and crush the garlic. Add to the bowl with the shrimp (prawns), sweet potato and cilantro (coriander) and mix together. Season with salt and pepper.

3. To make the dip, stir the sweet chili sauce and soy sauce together and put in a serving bowl.

4. Form the sweet potato and shrimp mixture into patties. Heat the oil in a skillet (frying pan), add the potato cakes and fry over a low heat for 2–3 minutes on each side until browned.

5. To serve, garnish with mint springs and lime wedges and serve with the dip.

THAI SHRIMP
WITH LETTUCE

Ingredients

2 tbsp sesame oil

1 lb 2 oz / 500 g ready-to-cook shrimp or king prawns, (fresh or frozen)

1 bunch fresh cilantro (coriander), finely chopped

1 garlic clove, finely chopped

1 lime, juiced

1 tsp honey

Salt & freshly ground pepper

1 round lettuce

Method
Prep and cook time: 20 min

1. Heat the sesame oil and fry the (thawed) shrimp on both sides for about 2 minutes. Add the cilantro (coriander) and the garlic and briefly fry together. Add the lime juice and season with salt, pepper and honey.

2. Arrange the salad and the shrimp in dishes. Serve garnished with cilantro.

ROAST DUCK SALAD

Ingredients

2 duck breasts, each about
14 oz / 400 g

1 tbsp clarified butter or oil

4 scallions (spring onions)

2 red chilies

14 oz / 400 g string beans

14 oz / 400 g sugarsnap peas

4 tbsp plum sauce

2 tbsp white wine vinegar

2 tbsp lime juice

Salt & freshly milled pepper

½ bunch basil, for garnish

Method

Prep and cook time: 40 min

1. Season the duck with salt and pepper and fry in the hot clarified butter. Fry on the skin side for about 10 minutes and on the other side for about 8 minutes. Take out of the skillet, wrap in aluminum foil and leave for about 10 minutes to rest.

2. Cut the white end of the scallions (spring onions) into thin rings, the green end into slightly thicker rings. Remove the seeds from the chilies and finely chop. Trim the string beans and the sugarsnap peas and blanch them in boiling, salted water for about 4–5 minutes.

3. Take the duck breasts out of the foil, carefully cut off the skin and cut the meat into thin slices. Arrange on 4 pre-warmed plates together with the vegetables and herbs.

4. Mix the plum sauce with the vinegar and the lime juice, drizzle over the salad and serve with freshly milled pepper, and garnished with basil leaves.

THAI SHRIMP AND PEANUT SALAD

Ingredients

7 oz / 200 g shrimp (or prawns), ready-prepared

1 fresh red chili pepper

2–3 garlic cloves

1 piece of ginger, about 1½ inches / 4 cm long

4 tbsp peanuts, chopped

4 tbsp oil

²/3 cup / 150 ml fish broth (stock)

Salt & freshly milled pepper

2 good pinches chili powder

2 tbsp soy sauce

1 tbsp oyster sauce

1 lime, juiced

½ bunch cilantro (coriander)

2 cups / 200 g glass noodles

Method

Prep and cook time: 25 min

1. Deseed the chili pepper and finely chop. Peel and finely chop the garlic and ginger. Toast the peanuts in a dry skillet, then place on one side.

2. Heat the oil and gently cook the chili, garlic and ginger for 3- 4 minutes until softened.

3. Increase the heat and add the shrimp, then pour in the fish broth (stock) and simmer for about 4 minutes. Season with salt, pepper, chili powder, soy sauce, oyster sauce and the juice from 1 lime.

4. Roughly chop the cilantro (coriander).

5. Pour boiling water over the glass noodles and leave for about 6 minutes. Drain, rinse with boiling hot water and drain again. Stir the noodles into the shrimp sauce. Add the roughly chopped cilantro.

6. Garnish with toasted peanuts and serve.

SWEET AND SOUR CHICKEN SALAD

Ingredients

For the dressing:

2 tbsp honey

4 tbsp olive oil

Finely grated zest and juice
of 1 orange

2 tbsp sweet chili sauce

Salt and freshly ground pepper, to taste

For the salad:

4 cooked smoked chicken breasts,
cut into chunks

2 cups / 400 g drained canned or
thawed frozen corn kernels

1 cucumber, cut into bite-size chunks

2 tomatoes, deseeded and diced

1 clementine / mandarin orange, peeled
and segmented

1 large carrot, sliced into matchsticks

5 oz / 150 g mixed salad greens

Deep fried rice noodles
(rice sticks), to garnish

Method

Prep and cook time: 25 min

1. To make the dressing spoon the honey
into a small jar with a tightly fitting lid. Add
the oil, orange zest and juice and sweet chili
sauce. Season with salt and ground black
pepper and shake to mix.

2. Place the chicken, corn, cucumber,
tomatoes, clementine (mandarin orange),
carrots and salad leaves into large bowl. Toss
together.

3. Drizzle with the dressing and garnish
with the rice noodles.

WAKAME, WATER CHESTNUT AND ORANGE SALAD

Ingredients

¾ oz / 20 g dried wakame seaweed

1 cucumber, seeded and cut into thin strips

1½ cups / 150 g snow peas (mangetout) cut into thin strips

1 inch / 3 cm piece fresh ginger root, peeled and finely grated

1 cup / 200 g canned sliced water chestnuts, drained

2 oranges

5 tbsp rice vinegar

1 tbsp sugar

½ tsp light soy sauce

Pinch salt

To garnish:

1 red chili pepper, seeded and finely chopped (wear gloves to prevent irritation)

4 tsp sesame seeds

Method
Prep and cook time: 1 hour

1. Put the wakame into a bowl and add enough warm water to cover. Soak until softened, about 15 minutes.

2. Put the cucumber in a colander and sprinkle with about 1 tsp salt. Leave for 10 minutes to soften.

3. Drain the wakame, cut off and discard any hard spines and chop lengthwise. Return to the bowl and add the snow peas (mangetout), ginger and water chestnuts.

4. Use a small sharp knife or vegetable peeler to remove orange peel, scraping off all traces of white pith. Remove the flesh from the

orange membranes, catching and reserving any juice. Halve the orange segments and add to the bowl along with the juice.

5. Rinse the cucumber and squeeze out the excess water; add to the salad bowl.

6. To prepare the dressing, put the sugar, rice vinegar and soy sauce into a small jar with a tight-fitting lid; add the salt and shake to blend. Drizzle over the salad and leave to marinate for 30 minutes.

7. Garnish with some chopped red chili and serve with a sprinkling of sesame seeds.

GLASS NOODLES WITH CHICKEN

Ingredients

2 cups / 200 g glass noodles

3 or 4 kaffir lime leaves

12 oz / 350 g chicken breast fillet

2 scallions (spring onions)

2 inches / 5 cm ginger, finely chopped

1 or 2 cloves garlic, finely chopped

3 or 4 shallots, finely chopped

2 red chilies, deseeded and finely chopped (wear gloves)

2 tbsp sesame oil

2 tbsp brown sugar

Juice of 2 limes

Salt & pepper

1 small cucumber, peeled and thinly sliced

2 handfuls herbs (e.g. mint, cilantro (coriander), Thai basil)

To garnish:

2 limes, halved

1/3 cup / 50 g unsalted peanuts, roasted

Method
Prep and cook time: 40 min

1. Soak the glass noodles in lukewarm water and cut into smaller lengths with scissors.

2. In a small pan heat about 4 cups (1 liter) water with the kaffir lime leaves and 1 teaspoon salt. Add the chicken breast and simmer gently over a low heat until cooked (about 12–15 minutes). Drain, let the meat cool slightly, then tear into small pieces.

2. Drain the glass noodles and cook in salted water, then refresh in cold water and drain well.

3. Peel and shred the scallions (spring onions). Soak in cold water.

3. Heat the oil in a skillet and sauté the ginger, garlic, shallots and chilies for 2–3 minutes. Stir in the sugar, sauté briefly, then add the glass noodles, chicken and lime juice. Season with pepper, mix well and set aside.

4. Drain the scallions and mix them into the chicken and noodles along with the cucumber and herbs. Pile the salad on plates and serve garnished with lime and scattered with peanuts.

ORIENTAL SALAD WITH SHRIMP

Ingredients

7 oz / 200 g cellophane noodles

2 tbsp vegetable oil, divided

8 jumbo shrimp (king prawns)

1–2 cloves garlic, minced

2 tbsp lime juice, divided

2 eggs, beaten

½ cup / 50 g bean sprouts

1–2 scallions (spring onions), chopped into 2-inch (5-cm) pieces (reserve a few for garnish)

¼ cup chopped roasted peanuts

4 slices pickled red ginger, chopped

1–2 tbsp rice vinegar

Fish sauce, to taste

Chili sauce, to taste

Salt and pepper

Method

Prep and cook time: 40 min

1. Put the cellophane noodles into a bowl, pour plenty of boiling water over them and let stand until softened, 10 minutes. Drain. Cut the noodles into smaller lengths.

2. Heat 1 tablespoon of the oil in a wok or skillet and quickly stir-fry the shrimp (prawns) and garlic. Sprinkle with 1 tbsp lime juice and set aside.

3. Heat the rest of the oil in a small skillet and scramble the eggs.

4. Mix the cellophane noodles with the bean sprouts, scallions (spring onions), scrambled eggs, peanuts and ginger. Divide onto plates.

5. In a small bowl whisk the rice vinegar, the rest of the lime juice, fish sauce, chili sauce, salt and white pepper; sprinkle over the salad. Put the shrimp on top of the salad and garnish with the reserved slivered scallions.

CHICKEN SALAD WITH MINT LEAVES

Ingredients

For the curry paste:

2 chilies

1 shallot

½ tsp freshly grated ginger

1 tsp shrimp paste

For the salad:

1 bunch scallions
(spring onions)

12 oz / 400 g mixed
salad leaves

1 handful mint leaves

1 handful cilantro
(coriander) leaves

1 onion

2 tomatoes

1 lb / 450 g chicken legs,
skinned and boned

1 tsp finely grated lemongrass

2 tbsp oil

For the dressing:

1 tbsp brown sugar

2 tbsp fish sauce

2 tbsp lime juice

Lemongrass, finely shredded
lengthways, to garnish

cilantro (coriander) leaves,
to garnish

Mint leaves, to garnish

Method
Prep and cook time: 30 min

1. Put all the curry paste ingredients into a mortar and grind to a paste.

2. Trim the scallions (spring onions) and cut into rings. Put the salad leaves into a bowl with the roughly chopped herbs and scallions (spring onions). Mix. Peel and dice the onion. Cut the tomatoes into wedges.

3. Cut the chicken into strips and put into a bowl with 2 tablespoons of the curry paste and the lemongrass. Mix. Heat the oil, brown

the meat on all sides then stir-fry for about 2 minutes. Take out of the skillet and sauté the diced onion in the oil.

4. Add the tomatoes and fry briefly, then return the meat to the skillet and cook gently until cooked through. Put the chicken, tomatoes and onion on top of the salad.

5. Heat the sugar, fish sauce and lime juice in the skillet. Drizzle over the salad. Serve garnished with lemongrass and herbs.

NOODLE SALAD WITH SHRIMP

Ingredients

9 oz / 250 g udon noodles

3 tbsp vegetable oil

12 oz / 300 g large shrimp (prawns), peeled and tail removed

2 tbsp light soy sauce

2 tbsp sesame oil

Juice of 1 lime

½ tsp sugar

2 handfuls arugula (rocket)

½ cucumber, seeds removed and chopped

4 scallions (spring onions), chopped

4 tbsp sesame seeds, lightly toasted

Method

Prep and cook time: 30 min

1. Cook the noodles according to the packet instructions, drain well and rinse under cold running water.

2. Heat the vegetable oil in a wok or skillet and stir fry the shrimp until they are cooked through. Remove from the wok and set aside.

3. Mix together the soy sauce, sesame oil, lime juice and sugar to make a dressing.

4. Mix the noodles, shrimp, arugula (rocket), cucumber and scallions (spring onions) in a large bowl and stir in the dressing.

5. Pile the salad onto serving plates and scatter with the sesame seeds.

FRIED FISH ON MANGO SALAD

Ingredients

4 sea bass fillets, each weighing about 5 oz / 150 g

2 green mangoes

1 shallot

2 red Thai chilies

Juice of ½ a lime

1 tbsp brown sugar

Fish sauce

⅓ cup / 50 g peanuts, chopped

2 tbsp flour

Oil for deep-frying

Method

Prep and cook time: 45 min

1. Peel the mangoes, cut the flesh away from the stone and shred. Peel and finely dice the shallot. Wash the chili, halve lengthways, remove the seeds and shred the flesh. Mix the mango with the shallot, chili, lime juice and brown sugar. Add fish sauce to taste and let the salad stand for about 20 minutes.

2. Toast the chopped peanuts in a dry frying pan until golden brown.

3 Dust the fish fillets with flour. Heat the oil and fry the fish for 3–4 minutes, or until cooked. Drain on paper towels.

4. Put the salad on plates, place a piece of fish on top of each serving of salad and serve sprinkled with peanuts.

SPICY NOODLE SALAD

Ingredients

1 carrot

1 cucumber

2 shallots

½ cup / 50 g bean sprouts

3 red chilies

7 oz / 200 g rice noodles

Cilantro (coriander) and mint leaves, shredded

For the Nuoc Cham Sauce:

5 garlic cloves, chopped very finely

5 red chilies, deseeded and very finely chopped

3½ tbsp Vietnamese fish sauce

Scant ½ cup / 100 ml water

3½ tbsp rice vinegar

¼ cup / 50 g sugar

Juice of 1 large lemon

Method

Prep and cook time: 25 min

1. Peel and halve the carrot and cucumber. Remove the cucumber seeds, cut the cucumber in half and cut lengthways into long, very thin strips. Cut the carrot into long very thin sticks. Peel the shallots and slice thinly. Wash and drain the soybean sprouts. Halve and deseed the chilies and cut into rings. Reserve a couple of chili rings to garnish.

2. Cook the noodles in boiling, salted water for about 2 minutes. Then drain, refresh in cold water and drain thoroughly. Set aside.

3. For the sauce, put all the ingredients apart from the lemon juice into a pan and heat, but do not let it boil. Then remove from heat and let cool. Stir in the lemon juice when the sauce is cold.

4. Put the noodles, cucumber, carrots, shallots, chilies and 6 tbsp of Nuoc Cham sauce into a large bowl and mix. Serve sprinkled with herbs and the reserved chili rings.

ROAST BEEF SALAD

Ingredients

1 lb 6 oz / 600 g well hung beef sirloin

1 tbsp clarified butter or oil

Salt & freshly ground pepper

8 oz / 200 g mixed salad leaves

4 small tomatoes

1 red onion

1 bunch cilantro (coriander) leaves

For the dressing:

2 tbsp white wine vinegar

1 tsp raspberry vinegar

4 tbsp olive oil

1 tsp sugar

½ tsp mustard

Salt

About ¼ tsp chili powder

Orange zest, to garnish

Method

Prep and cook time: 50 min

1. Preheat the oven to 325°F (160°C / Gas Mark 3). Trim the beef. Heat the clarified butter in an ovenproof skillet and brown the meat on both sides over a very high heat. Season with salt and pepper, place in a roasting dish and roast in the oven for 20–30 minutes (depending how well-done you like your meat). Take out and let rest for 5 minutes before carving.

2. Quarter the tomatoes. Peel the onion and cut into wedges. Put the salad leaves, tomato, onion and cilantro (coriander) leaves into a bowl. Reserve some cilantro leaves for garnishing.

3. For the dressing, mix all the dressing ingredients, check the seasoning, add to the prepared salad ingredients and toss.

4. Slice the roast beef thinly. Divide the salad between 4 plates and arrange the beef on top.

5. Serve garnished with cilantro leaves and orange zest.

THAI SOY DIP

Ingredients

2 scallions (spring onions)

1 garlic clove

1 red chili pepper

½ tsp grated ginger

²/3 cup / 150 ml soy sauce

1 tbsp sesame oil

½ tbsp honey

Method

Prep and cook time: 10 min

1 Slice the scallions (spring onions) into long, very narrow strips (about 1 inch / 3 cm).

2 Peel and finely chop the garlic clove.

3 Cut the chili pepper in half. Remove the seeds and ribs and slice into strips.

4 Mix together the pepper, scallions, garlic, ginger, soy sauce, oil and honey.

CHILI CORIANDER DRESSING

Ingredients

1 red chili pepper

1 green chili pepper

½ cup / 10 g cilantro (coriander) leaves

½ cup / 10 g fresh Thai basil

2 garlic cloves, peeled

8 tsp / 40 ml rice vinegar

2 tbsp soy sauce

¹/3 cup / 75 ml vegetable oil

Salt

Method

Prep and cook time: 10 min

1 Slice the chilies in half, lengthwise. Remove the ribs and seeds.

2 Put the chilies, cilantro (coriander), basil, garlic cloves, vinegar, soy sauce and half of the oil in a food processor and make a fine purée.

3 Mix in the remaining oil and season with salt to taste.

SWEET CHILI SAUCE

Ingredients

4 red chili peppers

2 cloves garlic, peeled and minced

Walnut sized piece fresh ginger, grated

½ cup / 125 ml water

7 tbsp / 100 ml white wine vinegar

1½ cups / 300 g sugar

½ tsp salt

Method
Prep and cook time: 40 min

1. Remove most of the seeds from the chili peppers and chop the flesh very finely.

2. Put all the ingredients into a pan and bring to a boil.

3. Cook gently for approx 30 minutes, stirring frequently, until the sauce is thick and glossy.

SPICY MARINADE

Ingredients

½ tsp each of: coriander seeds, peppercorns and cumin

1 tsp salt

½ tsp dried thyme

1 tsp paprika powder

2½ tsp sugar

1 tsp chili powder

1 tsp mustard powder

7 tbsp / 100 ml sunflower oil

Method
Prep and cook time: 10 min

1. Coarsely crush the coriander seeds, peppercorns, cumin and salt in a mortar.

2. Combine the crushed spices with the thyme, paprika powder, sugar, chili powder, mustard powder and sunflower oil.

3. Use to marinade and baste steaks, lamb or pork.

MAIN DISHES

MEAT AND POULTRY

LAMB IN SPINACH SAUCE

Ingredients

1 cup / 250 ml yogurt

2 tsp ground coriander

1 tsp each: ground cumin, curcuma (turmeric) and chili powder

1 tsp salt

1 lb 8 oz / 650 g lamb, from the leg, cut into chunks

4 tbsp clarified butter or oil

1 onion, finely chopped

2 garlic cloves, chopped

Thumb size piece ginger, peeled and finely chopped

Juice of 1 lime

2 handfuls spinach, washed and roughly chopped

To serve:

Fresh ginger, peeled and cut into thin matchsticks

1 tsp paprika

Method

Prep and cook time: 1 hour plus
1 hour to marinate

1. Mix the yogurt with the coriander, cumin, curcuma (turmeric), chili powder and salt in a large bowl. Add the lamb and set aside to marinate for 1 hour.

2. Heat the butter in a wide pan and gently fry the onion until soft but not brown. Add the garlic and ginger, cook for 1 minute then add the meat and the marinade.

3. Simmer very gently for 45 minutes or until the meat is tender. Add the lime juice and spinach and cook for a further 5 minutes.

4. Serve with the ginger matchsticks and paprika sprinkled over.

HOT AND SOUR LAMB

Ingredients

4 tbsp vegetable oil or ghee

2 onions, very finely chopped

2 garlic cloves, finely chopped

1 red chili, deseeded and finely chopped

1 tsp ground cinnamon

2 tbsp mustard seeds

Thumb-size piece fresh ginger, peeled and grated

1 tsp ground cumin

2 lb 8 oz / 1.5 g lamb, cut into large chunks

2 tomatoes, deseeded and chopped

½ cup / 125 ml white wine vinegar

Chopped parsley, to garnish

Method

Prep and cook time: 1 hour 45 min

1. Heat the oil in a large pan and gently cook the onions until soft. Stir in the garlic, chili, cinnamon, mustard seeds, ginger and cumin and cook for 2 more minutes.

2. Turn the heat up and add the lamb. Brown the meat on all sides then add the tomatoes and vinegar and season with salt and pepper. Pour in about 1 cup of water and simmer very gently for about 1¼ hours, stirring frequently, or until the meat is very tender. Add more water if needed during the cooking but bear in mind the finished dish should be fairly dry.

3. Serve with rice and garnished with chopped parsley.

LAMB SHANK WITH PRUNES AND APRICOTS

Ingredients

4 lamb shanks

1 stalk celery

1 leek

2 carrots

2 onions

2 cloves garlic

3–4 oz / 100 g prunes, pitted

3–4 oz / 100 g dried apricots, pitted

2 oz / 50 g ghee or clarified butter

2 bay leaves

2 sprigs fresh thyme

2 sprigs fresh rosemary

14 fl oz / 400 ml dry white wine

14 fl oz / 400 ml lamb broth (stock)

7 fl oz / 200 g light (single) cream

1–2 tbsp yellow mild curry powder

1–2 tbsp cornstarch (cornflour)

Salt & freshly milled pepper

Method

Prep and cook time: 3 hours 30 min

1. Pre-heat the oven to 300°F (150°C / Gas Mark 2). Cut some of the fat off the lamb shanks, then season with salt and pepper. Trim the celery and leek and roughly chop. Peel and roughly chop the carrots, onions and garlic.

2. Soak the prunes and apricots in lukewarm water.

3. Heat the ghee or clarified butter in a roasting pan and fry the lamb shanks on all sides until browned. Remove the meat, then fry the prepared vegetables and add the bay leaves and the herbs. Fry over a high heat until browned, stirring continually. Pour in the wine and reduce until the liquid has almost evaporated. Now pour in the lamb broth (stock) and place the lamb shanks in the roasting pan again. Cover and roast in the pre-heated oven for about 2½ hours. Add a little water or broth if necessary.

4. Remove the meat from the roasting pan, cover and keep warm.

5. Strain the pan juices through a fine-mesh sieve. Spoon off some of the fat, drain the apricots and the prunes, add them to the meat juices and bring to a boil. Pour in the cream, stir in the curry powder and simmer for about 10 minutes. Mix the cornstarch (cornflour) with a few drops of cold water until smooth then stir into the sauce to thicken. Season with salt and pepper and serve with the lamb shanks.

LAMB WITH SPICED RICE

Ingredients

2 lb 4 oz / 1 kg lamb, e.g. shoulder

3 tbsp ghee or clarified butter

2 onions, diced

2 cloves garlic, finely chopped

1 tsp curcuma (turmeric)

1 tbsp paprika, noble sweet

Spice mixture: 1 good pinch each of ground: cumin, coriander seeds, allspice, cloves and cinnamon

1 cup / 250 g yogurt

For the rice:

1¼ cups / 250 g basmati rice

4 cardamom pods

4 cloves

1 cinnamon stick

2 fresh bay leaves

1 tsp curcuma (turmeric)

For the yogurt sauce:

1¾ cups / 400 g yogurt

Juice of 1 lemon

1 tbsp mint leaves, chopped

Salt

Method
Prep and cook time: 2 hours

1. Cut the lamb into large cubes.

2. Heat the ghee (or clarified butter) and brown the meat over a fairly high heat. Add the onions, garlic and spices. Deglaze with a little water and add the yogurt. Cover and cook in the oven at 350°F (180°C / Gas Mark 4) for about 1½ hours. Stir occasionally and add more water if necessary.

3. Meanwhile, put the rice into a pan with the spices. Add double the amount of water,

cover and bring to a boil. Simmer for about 25 minutes, until cooked.

4. For the yogurt sauce, mix all the ingredients and season to taste with salt.

5. Take the lid off the curry and let brown for about 10 minutes. Check the seasoning and serve with the rice, the yogurt sauce and poppadoms.

LAMB SAAG

Ingredients

1 onion, roughly chopped

3 garlic cloves

Thumb-size piece ginger, peeled and roughly chopped

2 green chili peppers, deseeded and roughly chopped

½ cup / 125 ml vegetable oil

2 lbs / 900 g lamb shoulder, cut into large chunks

2 tsp coriander seeds, crushed

2 cardamom pods, crushed

1 tsp cumin seeds, crushed

1 tsp garam masala

1 tsp curcuma (turmeric)

1 tsp salt

1 tbsp tomato paste (purée)

1 cup / 250 ml lamb broth (stock) or water

2 large handfuls spinach, washed and roughly chopped

Method
Prep and cook time: 1 hour 30 min

1. Put the onion, garlic, ginger and chili peppers in a food processor and blend to make a purée.

2. Heat the oil in a wide pan and brown the meat pieces on all sides. Remove from the pan and set aside.

3. Fry the spices in the oil for 2 minutes then add the salt and onion purée and cook for 3 minutes.

4. Return the meat to the pan, add the tomato paste (purée) and lamb broth (stock) then simmer with a lid on very gently for about 45 minutes. Add a little water during the cooking if needed.

5. Add the spinach to the pan and cook for a further 30 minutes or until the lamb is very tender.

GROUND LAMB, POTATO AND SPINACH CURRY

Ingredients

5 tbsp clarified butter or oil

2 garlic cloves, finely chopped

2 tsp garam masala

1 tsp ground coriander

1 tsp ground cumin

1 lb / 450 g ground (minced) lamb

Salt and pepper

2 onions, sliced

Thumb-size piece ginger, finely chopped

1 red chili pepper, deseeded and finely chopped

1 tsp curcuma (turmeric)

6 large potatoes, peeled and cut into chunks

2 cups / 500 ml meat broth (stock)

1 cup / 250 ml yogurt

2 large handfuls spinach, washed and roughly chopped

Method

Prep and cook time: 1 hour

1. Heat 3 tbsp of the butter in a wide pan and fry the garlic, garam masala, coriander and cumin for 2 minutes.

2. Add the lamb and fry for 5 minutes or until the lamb is browned all over then pour in about a cup of water and cook with a lid on for about 15 minutes, stirring from time to time. Remove the lid, cook until the water has evaporated then season with salt and pepper and set aside.

3. Heat the remaining butter a clean pan and gently fry the onions for 2 minutes. Add the ginger, chili pepper and curcuma (turmeric) and cook for 2 more minutes.

4. Add the potatoes, stir for 2 minutes to coat the potatoes with the spices then pour in the meat broth (stock). Bring to a boil then turn the heat down and add the yogurt. Season with salt and pepper and simmer very gently for 15 minutes or until the potatoes are tender.

5. Wilt the spinach in a pan with a splash of water then drain and squeeze out the excess moisture.

6. To serve, place the cooked lamb onto warmed serving dishes, top with the spinach and pour over the onion and potato mixture.

ROAST LAMB WITH INDIAN SPICES

Ingredients

1 small leg of lamb

2 tsp coriander seeds

2 tbsp cumin seeds

1 onion, roughly chopped

²/₃ cup / 50 g flaked almonds

2 garlic cloves

Thumb-size piece of fresh ginger, peeled and grated

2 green chilies, deseeded and chopped

2 tsp salt

2 cups / 500 ml yogurt

2 tbsp vegetable oil

1 tsp ground curcuma (turmeric)

1 tsp cayenne pepper

1 tsp garam masala

3 strips cassia bark or cinnamon

Method

Prep and cook time: 2 hours plus 24 hours to marinate

1. Score the skin of the lamb with a sharp knife.

2. Toast the coriander and cumin seeds in a dry skillet until lightly browned then grind to a powder with a pestle and mortar.

3. Put the ground seeds, onion, almonds, garlic, ginger, chilies and salt into a food processor with 3 tbsp yoghurt and blend to make a paste.

4. Heat the oil in a skillet and gently fry the curcuma (turmeric), cayenne and garam masala for 2 minutes. Stir in the paste and add the rest of the yogurt. Rub the mixture all over the lamb, cover and marinate in the refrigerator for 24 hours.

5. Remove the meat from the refrigerator 1 hour before you want to cook it. Heat the oven to 400F (200C / Gas Mark 6).

6. Transfer the lamb to a roasting pan and spread all the yogurt marinade over it. Tuck the cassia bark under the meat, cover with kitchen foil and roast for 1 hour.

7. Remove the foil, baste and cook a further 30 minutes. Let the meat rest for 15 minutes before serving.

LAMB BIRYANI

Ingredients

1½ lb / 650 g lamb (leg)

7 tbsp ghee or clarified butter

1–2 onions, finely diced

2 tsp freshly grated ginger

3 cloves garlic, pressed

6 cardamom pods

5 cloves

1 piece cinnamon stick (¾-1 inch / 2–3 cm)

½ tsp ground cumin

½ tsp curcuma (turmeric)

chili powder, to taste

⅔ cup / 150 g yogurt

⅔ cup / 150 ml meat broth (stock)

Salt

1½ cups / 300 g basmati rice

⅓ cup / 50 g raisins

4 tbsp milk

A few saffron threads

6 tbsp blanched almonds

Cilantro (coriander) leaves, to garnish

Method
Prep and cook time: 2 hours 15 min

1. Preheat the oven to 350°F (180°C / Gas Mark 4).

2. Cut the meat into bite-size pieces. Heat 4 tablespoons ghee (or clarified butter) in a pan and sauté half of the onions until translucent. Add the ginger, cardamom, garlic, cloves, cinnamon and meat and fry, stirring frequently, until the meat is lightly browned on all sides. Stir in the ground spices, yogurt and broth (stock) and season with salt. Cover and simmer over a low heat for 45–60 minutes, stirring occasionally (it will be very thick).

3. Sauté the rest of the onions in a pan without letting them color. Wash the rice in a sieve under running water and add to the onions with just double the amount of lightly salted water. Bring to a boil and cook, covered, over a very low heat for about 5 minutes.

4. Put the meat into a greased baking dish. Drain the rice and mix with the raisins. Heat the milk, add the saffron and 2 tablespoons ghee and let them dissolve. Add the milk to the rice and mix with the meat in the dish.

5. Put a lid on the dish (or seal with aluminum foil) and cook on the middle shelf of the preheated oven for about 1 hour.

6. Lightly toast the almonds in the remaining ghee and add to the dish.

7. Before serving fluff up the lamb biryani with a fork, season to taste and spoon onto plates. Scatter some cilantro (coriander) over the top and serve.

MUGHLAI LAMB KORMA

Ingredients

1 cup / 250 ml full-fat yogurt

1 tsp salt

2 tsp ground cumin

1 tsp ground coriander

A pinch of cayenne pepper

Freshly milled pepper

4 tbsp freshly chopped cilantro (coriander)

5 tbsp olive oil

1 bay leaf

6 cardamom pods

Cinnamon stick (2 inches / about 5 cm)

2 lb / 900 g lamb, from the shoulder, without bones, cut into bite-size cubes

1 onion, chopped

4 tbsp golden raisins

2 tbsp sour cream

A pinch of ground cardamom

Method

Prep and cook time: 1 hour 30 min

1. Mix the yogurt with the salt, cumin, ground coriander, cayenne pepper, black pepper and fresh cilantro (coriander) leaves and set aside.

2. Heat the oil in a large skillet. When the oil is hot add the bay leaf, cardamom pods, cinnamon and diced meat. Brown the meat on all sides over a medium heat. If the skillet is not big enough to take all the meat at once, fry the meat a few pieces at a time so that it has plenty of room in the pan.

3. Take the meat out of the skillet and keep warm. Sauté the onion until translucent in the oil left in the pan.

4. Return the meat to the skillet with the spices, add the yogurt mixture and golden raisins and bring to a boil. Cover and cook over a low heat for 60–70 minutes, until the meat is very tender. Then remove the lid and cook over a high heat until the sauce is reduced to the desired consistency.

5. Stir in the sour cream, season with the ground cardamom and serve at once.

LAMB ROGAN JOSH

Ingredients

6 tbsp vegetable oil

2¼ lbs / 1kg lamb, cut into large chunks

1 onion, chopped

4 garlic cloves, chopped

Thumb-size piece fresh ginger, peeled and chopped

1 tsp ground cinnamon

2 tsp ground cumin

2 tsp ground coriander

1 tsp chili powder

2 tbsp tomato paste (purée)

2 cups / 400 g canned tomatoes, chopped

Salt and pepper

Cilantro (fresh coriander), to garnish

Method

Prep and cook time: 1 hour 30 min

1. Heat 4 tbsp of the oil in a large pan and fry the lamb pieces until browned all over. Remove the meat from the pan and set aside.

2. Heat the remaining oil in the pan and gently cook the onion until softened. Add the garlic and the spices and cook for 2 minutes.

3. Stir in the tomato paste (purée) and return the meat to the pan. Add the canned tomatoes, season with salt and pepper and cook very gently, stirring from time to time, for about 1¼ hours or until the meat is very tender. You might need to add a little water during cooking to prevent the sauce from becoming too dry.

SPICED LAMB WITH CHICKPEAS

Ingredients

3 tbsp clarified butter or oil

1 lb 8 oz / 600 g lamb, from the leg, cubed

1 onion, finely chopped

2 garlic cloves, chopped

1 red chili pepper, deseeded and finely chopped

2 tsp garam masala

1 tsp ground coriander

1 tsp cumin

4 medium potatoes, peeled and cut into chunks

2 cups / 400 g canned tomatoes, chopped

½ cup / 125 ml lamb broth (stock) or water

2 cups / 400 g canned chickpeas, drained and rinsed

Salt and pepper

Method

Prep and cook time: 1 hour

1. Heat the butter in a deep pan and gently fry the lamb until browned all over.

2. Add the onion, garlic, chili pepper, garam masala, coriander and cumin and cook for 2 minutes.

3. Add the potatoes, stir for 1 minute then add the tomatoes and the lamb broth (stock). Season with salt and pepper and simmer very gently for 30 minutes. Add more water during cooking if needed.

4. Add the chickpeas and cook for 15 minutes more or until the lamb is very tender.

SPICY LAMB AND TOMATO CURRY

Ingredients

Thumb-size piece fresh ginger, peeled and chopped

1 tbsp garam masala

2 lbs / 900 g lean lamb, cut into large chunks

6 tbsp vegetable oil

4 onions, diced

2 garlic cloves, sliced

1 green chili pepper, deseeded and finely chopped

½ tsp ground cumin

1 tsp paprika

Salt and pepper

2 tbsp tomato paste (purée)

3 tomatoes, diced

8 sprigs cilantro (fresh coriander), leaves and stalks, finely chopped

4 tbsp yogurt

Method

Prep and cook time: 1 hour 20 min plus 30 min to marinate

1. Mix the ginger with the garam masala and rub into the lamb chunks. Marinate at room temperature for at least 30 minutes.

2. Heat 2 tbsp of oil in a large pan and fry the onion, garlic and chili pepper on a gentle heat until softened but not brown. Stir in the cumin and paprika and season with salt and pepper. Cook for 2 minutes then remove the mixture from the pan and set aside.

3. Heat 4 tbsp of oil in the pan and fry the lamb on a medium heat on all sides for 5 minutes.

4. Stir the tomato paste (purée) into the pan, add the onion mixture and pour over 3 cups / 750 ml water.

5. Bring to a boil then reduce the heat and cook very gently, stirring occasionally, for 1 hour or until the meat is tender.

6. Check the seasoning then divide between 4 bowls and garnish with the cilantro (coriander), diced tomatoes and yogurt.

INDIAN MEATBALLS

Ingredients

1 lb / 450 g ground (minced) lamb

2 scallions (spring onions), finely chopped

2 green chili peppers, deseeded and finely chopped

1 tsbp chopped cilantro (coriander) leaves, plus some to garnish

Salt and pepper

5 tbsp oil

2 onions, finely sliced

2 garlic cloves, finely chopped

Thumb-size piece ginger, peeled and grated

2 tsp garam masala

1 tsp coriander seeds, crushed

1 tsp cumin seeds, crushed

1 cup / 200 g canned tomatoes, chopped

Salt and pepper

Couscous, to serve

Method
Prep and cook time: 45 min

1. Mix the lamb with the scallions, chili peppers, cilantro (coriander), salt and pepper and shape into meatballs.

2. Heat 3 tbsp of oil in a wide skillet and fry the meatballs until browned all over. Remove from the skillet and set aside.

3. Heat the remaining oil in the skillet and fry the onions until soft but not brown. Add the garlic, ginger, garam masala, coriander, and cumin seeds and fry for 2 minutes.

4. Return the meatballs to the pan and add the tomatoes and about ½ cup water. Simmer very gently for 20 minutes or until the meatballs are cooked through. Season with salt and pepper.

5. Serve with couscous and garnish with the cilantro (coriander) leaves.

LAMB JALFREZI

Ingredients

4 tbsp clarified butter or oil

2 onions, finely sliced into rings

1 tsp cumin seeds

1 tsp black mustard seeds

1 tsp fenugreek seeds

2 tsp garam masala

1 green bell pepper, deseeded
and sliced

1 lb 8 oz / 650 g lamb, from the leg;
roughly chopped

Method
Prep and cook time: 25 min

1. Heat the butter in a wide skillet and fry
the onion rings until soft but not brown. Stir
in the cumin, black mustard, fenugreek and
garam masala and cook for 2 minutes.

2. Add the green bell pepper and cook for
2 minutes then turn up the heat and add the
lamb. Fry quickly, stirring all the time, for
5 minutes or until the lamb is cooked
through.

3. Serve with rice.

PORK WITH COCONUT AND GINGER SAUCE

Ingredients

5 tbsp vegetable oil

1 lb 8 oz / 650 g pork loin, cut into chunks

1 onion, very finely chopped

2 garlic cloves, finely chopped

Thumb-size piece fresh ginger, peeled and grated

Juice of 2 limes

2 cups / 500 ml coconut milk

Salt and pepper

To serve:

1 tbsp dried red chilies, crumbled

2 thumb-size pieces fresh ginger, peeled and cut into matchsticks

2/3 cup / 100 g cashew nuts, roughly chopped

Method

Prep and cook time: 35 min

1. Heat 3 tbsp of the oil in a wide skillet and fry the pork pieces for about 8 minutes, stirring from time to time, or until golden brown and cooked through. Remove the meat from the skillet, set aside and keep warm.

2. Meanwhile, heat the remaining oil in the skillet and gently fry the onion until soft but not brown. Add the garlic and ginger and cook for 1 more minute.

3. Sprinkle the lime juice into the skillet along with a splash of water, let it bubble for 1 minute and stir well. Pour in the coconut milk and simmer for about 15 minutes, stirring from time to time, or until the mixture has thickened and reduced by about a half. Season with salt and pepper.

4. To serve, stir the meat into the coconut mixture and place in warmed serving bowls. Sprinkle over the dried chilies, ginger matchsticks and cashew nuts and serve immediately.

SWEET AND SOUR PORK

Ingredients

1 tbsp rice wine

1 tbsp light soy sauce

2 tsp sesame oil

1 lb / 450 g pork loin, cut into cubes

1 egg, lightly beaten

4 tbsp cornstarch (cornflour), divided

Vegetable oil for deep-frying

For the sauce:

1 large carrot, sliced diagonally

$^2/_3$ cup / 150 ml chicken broth (stock)

1 tbsp light soy sauce

2 tsp dark soy sauce

2 tsp sesame oil

4 tsp rice vinegar

1 tbsp sugar

2 tbsp ketchup

2 tsp cornstarch (cornflour), mixed to a smooth paste in 1 tbsp water

1 red bell pepper, chopped into diamonds

4 scallions (spring onions), trimmed and roughly chopped

To garnish:

Cilantro (fresh coriander) leaves

Method
Prep and cook time: 40 min

1. Combine the rice wine, soy sauce and sesame oil in a medium bowl; add the pork and toss to coat. Let marinate for 15 minutes.

2. In a wide shallow bowl, beat the egg with 1 tbsp of the cornstarch (cornflour). Place the remaining 3 tbsp cornstarch in another wide shallow bowl.

3. Heat the oil in a deep fat fryer to 180°C / 350°F.

4. Lift the pork from the marinade and toss in the cornstarch to dredge. Then dip the pork into the egg-cornstarch mixture to coat.

5. Working in batches, deep-fry the pork for about 5 minutes or until golden. Drain on paper towels and keep warm.

6. For the sauce, cook the carrot in boiling water until softened, 2 minutes; drain and set aside.

7. In a large skillet or wok, combine the chicken broth (stock), light and dark soy sauce, sesame oil, rice vinegar, sugar, ketchup, and cornstarch and water mixture into a pan and bring to a boil. Cook, stirring, until slightly thickened.

8. Stir in the carrot, pepper and scallions (spring onions).

9. Add the fried pork and heat through, stirring gently. Serve at once, garnished with cilantro (coriander) leaves.

SPARE RIBS WITH SHIITAKE MUSHROOMS

Ingredients

For the spare ribs:

4 ½ lbs / 2 kg spare ribs

4 tbsp plum sauce

4 tbsp honey

4 tbsp soy sauce

Thumb-size piece fresh ginger, peeled and grated

4 tbsp sesame oil

4 tbsp rice vinegar

1 tsp five-spice powder

For the vegetables:

3 tbsp vegetable oil

1 tbsp butter

8 oz / 200 g shiitake mushrooms, stalks removed

2 red chili peppers, deseeded and finely chopped

2 cloves garlic, finely chopped

1 red bell pepper, deseeded and sliced

1 green bell pepper, deseeded and sliced

4 scallions (spring onions), sliced

½ cup / 50 g pine nuts

2 tbsp soy sauce

2 tbsp toasted sesame seeds, to garnish

Method

Prep and cook time: 1 hour 15 min plus 6 hours to marinate

1. For the spare ribs, place the ribs in a large pan of salted water, bring to a boil and simmer for 40 minutes or until the meat is tender. Drain well and place in a large bowl.

2. Combine the remaining ingredients for the ribs together and mix into the ribs, ensuring they are evenly coated. Set aside to marinate for at least 6 hours.

3. Heat the oven to 425°F (220°C / Gas Mark 7).

4. Place the ribs and the marinade in a roasting pan and roast in the oven for 15–20 minutes, basting from time to time.

5. Meanwhile, cook the vegetables. Heat the oil and butter in a wok or deep skillet and gently fry the mushrooms until they have softened. Turn the heat to high and add the chili peppers, garlic, bell peppers and scallions (spring onions).

6. Stir fry for 5 minutes then add the pine nuts and soy sauce.

7. Serve the ribs and vegetables with the sesame seeds scattered over.

BEAN CURRY
WITH PORK

Ingredients

1 lb 2 oz / 500 g green beans

14 oz / 400 g pork (escalope), diced

3–4 tbsp yellow curry paste

4 oz / 100 g bacon, cut into strips

1 lb 2 oz / 500 g cooked potatoes

2 tbsp oil

1 tbsp onion, diced

1¾ cups / 400 ml unsweetened coconut milk

Dill weed (dill), chopped

Red chili, chopped, to taste

Salt & pepper

Method

Prep and cook time: 30 min

1. Trim the beans and cut into pieces, then blanch in boiling salted water for 3–5 minutes. Refresh in ice-cold water and drain.

2. Mix the meat with the curry paste.

3. Peel and dice the potatoes.

4. Heat the oil in a deep skillet or wok, add the bacon and fry for 2–3 minutes. Then add the meat and onion and fry the meat on all sides, stirring constantly.

5. Pour in the coconut milk and the prepared vegetables. Bring to a boil, stirring occasionally, and simmer for 5 minutes. Add some dill weed, season with salt and pepper and add chili to taste. Spoon into bowls and serve garnished with more dill weed.

ROAST PORK WITH VEGETABLES

Ingredients

For the marinade:

4 tbsp light soy sauce

2 tbsp rice wine or dry sherry

2 tbsp hoisin sauce

2 cloves garlic, minced

1 inch / 3 cm piece fresh ginger root, peeled and grated

3 tbsp honey, divided

1 lb / 450 g pork loin

For the stir-fry:

2 tbsp sesame oil, divided

4 scallions (spring onions), thinly sliced

4 carrots, sliced into thin sticks

1 red bell pepper, cut into thin strips

7 oz / 200 g snow peas or sugar snap peas, sliced into thin strips

Method

Prep and cook time: 45 min plus 2 hours marinating

1. To prepare the marinade, mix together the soy sauce, rice wine or dry sherry, hoisin sauce, garlic, ginger and 1 tbsp of the honey in a medium bowl. Add the pork to the bowl and turn to coat well. Cover and marinate in the refrigerator for 2 hours.

2. Pre-heat the oven to 375°F (190°C / Gas Mark 5). Half fill a roasting pan with water and rest a rack on top.

3. In a small bowl, combine the remaining 2 tbsp of honey with 1 tbsp sesame oil and 3 tbsp of the marinade.

4. Put the pork onto the rack and brush with the honey-marinade mixture. Roast for 15 minutes, brush over more of the honey marinade and roast for 20 more minutes until the pork is cooked.

5. Meanwhile, heat the remaining 1 tbsp sesame oil in a large skillet or wok. Add the scallions, carrots, bell pepper and snow peas or sugar snaps and cook for 5 minutes until the vegetables are slightly softened but still crunchy.

6. Bring the remaining marinade to a boil and cook, stirring, until slightly reduced, 5 minutes.

7. Slice the pork and serve on a bed of vegetables with a little of the cooked marinade poured over.

PORK CURRY WITH TAMARIND

Ingredients

For the curry paste:

2 green chilies

1 tsp shrimp paste

1 tsp ground curcuma (turmeric)

1 tsp freshly grated ginger

For the curry:

2 oz / 50 g pressed tamarinds

2 onions

1 lb 6 oz / 600 g pork

2 tbsp fish sauce

2 tbsp oil

14 oz / 400 ml can unsweetened coconut milk

Salt

Sugar

½ bunch Thai basil, to garnish

Method

Prep and cook time: 55 min plus 30 min soaking time

1. Put all the curry paste ingredients into a mortar and grind to a paste.

2. Soak the tamarinds in ½ cup (120 ml) water for about 30 minutes. Peel and finely slice the onions. Cut the meat into bite-size cubes. Put into a bowl with the fish sauce and let stand for 10 minutes.

3. Heat the oil in a large skillet and brown the meat on all sides in batches. Take the creamy top of the coconut milk and put into a pan. Add the rest of the coconut milk to the skillet with the meat, cover and simmer for about 20 minutes.

4. Bring the coconut cream to a boil in the pan and simmer for 2 minutes. Add 2 tablespoons of the curry paste and stir until dissolved. Add the onions and cook for about 1 minute. Transfer the meat and coconut sauce from the skillet to the pan.

5. Squeeze out the tamarind, discard the fibers and add the liquid to the curry. Simmer for about 15 minutes, until the meat is cooked. Add salt and sugar to taste.

6. Garnish with Thai basil and serve.

PORK SATAY

Ingredients

For the satay:

1 lb 6 oz / 600 g pork,
such as escalopes

2 garlic cloves

1 chili, finely chopped

1 shallot, finely chopped

¼ tsp ground cumin

¼ tsp ground coriander

2 tbsp soy sauce

4 tbsp coconut milk

2 tbsp oil

Salt & pepper

For the peanut sauce:

1 cup / 150 g unsalted,
shelled peanuts

4 tbsp oil

1 shallot, chopped

2 tbsp peanut butter

1 tsp curry powder

1 dried red chili, crushed

1 lemon, juice and grated zest

Pinch of sugar

$1/3$ cup / 80 ml chicken
broth (stock)

Method

Prep and cook time: 25 min plus
2 hours marinating time

1. Cut the pork into thin strips about ¾ inch
(2 cm) wide.

2. Mix the rest of the ingredients to make a
marinade and marinate the strips of pork for
at least 2 hours.

3. Meanwhile, make the sauce, toast the
peanuts in a dry skillet, leave to cool.

4. Heat the oil and sauté the shallot until
translucent. Stir in the peanut butter, curry
powder, crushed peanuts and chili, lemon
juice and zest, and add sugar, salt and
pepper to taste. Then stir in enough chicken
broth (stock) to produce a creamy sauce.

5. Remove the pork from the marinade,
drain and thread lengthways on wooden
skewers. Grill on a hot grill for about
4 minutes, turning frequently until cooked
through (or fry in oil in a skillet). Serve with
the peanut sauce.

PORK WITH PLUM SAUCE

Ingredients

1 lb 12 oz / 800 g pork loin,
cut into strips

2 tsp sesame oil

2 carrots, peeled and sliced into
thin strips

1 clove garlic, minced

1 inch / 3-cm piece fresh ginger root,
peeled and grated

2 tbsp soy sauce, plus more to taste

2–3 tbsp plum sauce

Garnish:

1 scallion (spring onion), thinly sliced
on the diagonal

Chopped fresh parsley

Method

Prep and cook time: 25 min

1. Heat the oil in a wok or large skillet until
very hot. Add the pork and cook, turning
occasionally, until browned on all sides.

2. Add the carrots, garlic, ginger, soy sauce
and a little water; heat through.

3. Stir in the plum sauce and simmer for
3–4 minutes, stirring occasionally.

4. Season the meat with soy sauce and serve
garnished with the scallion (spring onion)
and parsley.

SPICY PORK VINDALOO

Ingredients

1 tbsp mustard oil

1 lb 12 oz / 800 g pork (e. g. shoulder), diced

2 onions, finely diced

2 cloves garlic, finely diced

1 tsp ginger, freshly grated

½ tsp cumin

½ tsp curcuma (tumeric)

1 stick cinnamon

1 lemon, juice

1 tsp tamarind paste

1 tsp brown sugar

1 new potato, to garnish

oil, for frying

Method

Prep and cook time: I hour

1. Heat the mustard oil and fry the meat in it. Add the onions, garlic and the spices and sauté.

2. Pour in the lemon juice, stir in the tamarind paste and sugar and add about $^2/_3$ cup (150 ml) of water. Cover and simmer gently over a low heat for 45–50 minutes. Add a little more water if needed.

3. For the garnish, slice the potato into very thin sticks and fry in hot oil until golden brown. Drain on a paper towel and lightly salt.

4. Season the curry, garnish with the potato sticks and serve.

PORK WITH VEGETABLES AND EGG FRIED RICE

Ingredients

1 tbsp sesame oil

1 inch / 3 cm piece fresh ginger root, grated

1 clove garlic, minced

1 red onion, sliced

1 lb / 450 g lean pork, cut into strips

1 red bell pepper, coarsely chopped

1 yellow bell pepper, coarsely chopped

4 oz / 100 g chestnut or brown button mushrooms, quartered

2 tbsp sweet chili sauce

2 tbsp dark soy sauce

2 tbsp teriyaki sauce

7 oz / 200 g snow peas (mangetout)

For the fried rice:

1 egg

2 tsp sesame oil

2 tbsp vegetable oil

1 cup / 200 g cooked long-grain rice

½ cup / 400 g thawed frozen peas

4 scallions (spring onions), finely chopped

Salt and freshly ground pepper, to taste

2 tsp light soy sauce

Method

Prep and cook time: 30 min

1. Heat the sesame oil in a large wok or skillet; add the ginger, garlic and onion, stir-fry for 2 minutes.

2. Add the pork and fry for 5 minutes, turning as needed, until browned. Add the red and yellow peppers and the mushrooms into the wok and cook, stirring, for another 5 minutes.

3. Pour in the sweet chili sauce, soy sauce and teriyaki sauce, then add the snow peas (mangetout). Cook for a further 2–3 minutes; set aside and keep warm.

4. For the fried rice, beat together the egg and sesame oil in a small bowl and set aside.

5. Heat the vegetable oil in a clean wok or skillet, then add the rice and stir-fry for about 3–4 minutes.

6. Add the peas and scallions (spring onions) and stir-fry for about 3 minutes. Season with salt and pepper and splash in the soy sauce, then push to one side of the wok.

7. Pour the beaten egg mixture into the other side of the wok and leave for about 10 seconds so it begins to set. Using a chopstick, briskly swirl around the egg to break it up, then toss it gently with the rice. Stir-fry for a further minute and serve at once with the pork and vegetables.

PORK RIBS WITH SCALLIONS AND CHILIES

Ingredients

3 lb / 1½ kg pork ribs (ask your butcher to chop into separate ribs)

Finely grated zest and juice of 2 oranges

3 tbsp soy sauce

2 tbsp tomato paste

2 tbsp vegetable oil

2 tbsp honey

1 inch / 3 cm piece fresh ginger root, peeled and grated

6 mild red chili peppers, slit open lengthwise and seeded

4 scallions (spring onions) green parts only; chopped into 2 inch / 5-cm strips

Method

Prep and cook time: 1 hour 20 min plus 2 hours to marinate

1. Bring a large pot of water to a boil. Place the ribs in the boiling water, reduce the heat and simmer until tender, around 45 minutes.

2. To prepare the marinade, in a small bowl, combine the orange zest and juice with the soy sauce, tomato paste, oil, honey and ginger.

3. Remove the ribs from the water and drain. Place in a shallow dish, pour over the marinade mixture and toss to coat well. Cover and marinate for at least 2 hours in the refrigerator.

4. Preheat the broiler (grill); line a broiler pan with foil and place the ribs on the broiler rack. Drizzle with the marinade and broil (grill) for around 10 minutes, until slightly crisped at the edges.

5. Turn the ribs, sprinkle with the chili peppers and scallions (spring onions) and continue broiling for a further 5–10 minutes.

PORK CURRY WITH FRESH HERBS

Ingredients

3 tbsp oil

1½ lb / 700 g lean pork (without skin or bones) diced

Salt & freshly milled pepper

1 onion, diced

1 dried chili, finely chopped

2 tsp finely grated fresh ginger

A good pinch of ground coriander

½ tsp ground curcuma (turmeric)

A good pinch of ground cumin

A pinch of ground cloves

2 tbsp dark soy sauce

1 tbsp chopped parsley

Scallion (spring onion) greens, cut into rings

Method

Prep and cook time: 1 hour

1. Heat the oil and quickly brown the meat on all sides. Season with salt and pepper and add the onion, ginger and chili. Fry gently for about 3 minutes.

2. Then stir in the coriander, curcuma (turmeric), cumin and cloves, and add ¾–1 cup / 200 ml of water and the soy sauce. Cover and cook for about 45 minutes.

3. Serve sprinkled with parsley and scallion (spring onion) rings.

PORK WITH GINGER AND CHILI

Ingredients

1½ lb / 800 g boned pork leg, trimmed of fat and cubed

3 tbsp vegetable oil

1 large onion, chopped

2 garlic cloves, finely chopped

1 red chili pepper, deseeded and finely sliced

Thumb-size piece fresh ginger, peeled and grated

½ tsp ground coriander

½ tsp ground curcuma (turmeric)

½ tsp ground cloves

½ tsp ground cumin

2 cups / 400 g canned tomatoes, chopped

²/₃ cup / 150 ml yogurt

Salt and pepper

2 tbsp chopped parsley, to garnish

Method

Prep and cook time: 1 hour 10 min

1. Heat the oil in a skillet (frying pan) and sear the meat on all sides until golden brown. Remove the meat from the pan and keep warm.

2. Add the onions to the pan, cook until softened but not brown then stir in the garlic, chili, ginger, coriander, curcuma (turmeric), cloves and cumin.

3. Cook the spices for 2 minutes then return the meat to the pan with the tomatoes and yogurt.

4. Season with salt and pepper then bring to a simmer and cook very gently for about 45 minutes or until the meat is tender. Add a little water during cooking if the dish looks too dry.

5. Serve sprinked with the parsley.

NOODLES WITH VEGETABLES AND PORK

Ingredients

4 oz / 100 g thin egg noodles

2 tbsp vegetable oil

12 oz / 350 g ground (minced) pork

Soy sauce, to taste

Cayenne pepper, to taste

1–2 tbsp sesame oil

2 cloves garlic, minced

2 scallions (spring onions), thinly sliced

1 inch / 3 cm fresh ginger root, peeled and finely chopped

7 oz / 200 g shiitake mushrooms, quartered

1 cup / 150 g snow peas (mangetout), halved diagonally

1 cup / 150 g thinly sliced Chinese cabbage leaves

2/3 cup / 150 g bamboo shoots, rinsed and drained

Method
Prep and cook time: 45 min

1. Cook the noodles in salted water according to package instructions. Rinse in a colander under running water; drain.

2. Heat the vegetable oil in a large skillet or wok; add the pork and cook, stirring constantly, until no longer pink. Season with soy sauce and cayenne, remove from the skillet and set aside to keep warm.

3. Return the skillet to the heat and add the sesame oil. Add the garlic, scallions (spring onions), ginger, mushrooms, snow peas (mangetout), cabbage and bamboo shoots and stir-fry for 2–3 minutes.

4. Add the reserved pork and noodles and continue frying for a further 2 minutes. Season to taste with additional soy sauce and cayenne and serve at once.

CHICKEN JALFREZI

Ingredients

1 lb 2 oz / 500 g chicken breast fillets

1 tbsp Worcestershire sauce

3 onions

7 oz / 200 g sugarsnap peas

1 cup / 150 g frozen peas

2 red chilies, or more
according to taste

3 tbsp oil

A good pinch of brown mustard seeds

A good pinch of cumin seeds

A good pinch of ground cumin

A pinch of ground coriander

A good pinch of ground curcuma
(turmeric)

$^2/_3$–$^3/_4$ cup / 150–200 ml coconut
cream, to taste

Salt & freshly milled pepper

Mint leaves

Method
Prep and cook time: 25 min

1. Cut the meat into thin strips and mix
with the Worcestershire sauce. Peel and
slice the onions. Trim the sugarsnap peas.
Thaw the frozen peas. Slit the chilies open
lengthways, remove the seeds and inner ribs,
and finely chop the flesh.

2. Heat the oil in a skillet and fry the
mustard seeds and cumin seeds, stirring, for
about 30 seconds, until they start to pop.
Add the onions and chilies and fry, stirring,
until the onions are lightly browned.

3. Stir in the meat, ground spices,
Worcestershire sauce, sugarsnap peas and
thawed frozen peas and season with salt and
pepper. Add 1 cup of water, bring to a boil
and cook over a medium heat for a further
3–5 minutes, stirring, until the meat and
vegetables are just cooked.

4. Add coconut cream to taste. Sprinkle
with mint and serve with rice.

FRUITY MANGO CHICKEN

Ingredients

4 tbsp clarified butter or oil

4 chicken thighs, cut in half through the bone

4 onions, sliced

2 garlic cloves, crushed

Thumb-size piece fresh ginger, peeled and grated

1 tsp curcuma (turmeric)

1 tsp paprika

1 tsp ground cumin

1 tsp ground coriander

1 cup / 250 ml chicken broth (stock)

1 cup / 250 ml coconut milk

1 cup / 200 g mango chutney

Juice of 1 lemon

Salt and pepper

1 red chili pepper, deseeded and finely sliced

Method

Prep and cook time: 50 min

1. Heat the butter in a wide pan and cook the chicken pieces until lightly browned all over. Remove from the pan and set aside.

2. Gently fry the onions until soft but not brown then add the garlic, ginger, curcuma (turmeric), paprika, cumin and coriander. Fry for 2 minutes, stirring all the time.

3. Return the chicken to the pan, stir to coat in the spices then pour in the chicken broth (stock) and coconut milk. Simmer gently for 20 minutes then add the mango chutney and lemon juice and season with salt and pepper.

4. Let simmer for another 15 minutes or until the chicken is cooked through. Serve with the sliced chili scattered over.

CHICKEN WITH ORANGE ZEST

Ingredients

2 oranges

2 cloves garlic, chopped

4 skinless boneless chicken breasts, cut into bite-size cubes

400 g / 1 lb glass (bean thread, cellophane) noodles

1 tbsp cornstarch (cornflour)

3 tbsp sesame oil

1 tbsp honey

Light soy sauce, to taste

Cayenne pepper, to taste

1 scallion (spring onion), green parts only, very thinly sliced on the diagonal, to garnish

Method

Prep and cook time: 30 min plus 12 hours to marinate

1. Finely grate the zest of one orange and remove the zest of the other in fine strips. Juice both oranges.

2. In a medium bowl, mix together the grated orange zest, orange juice and garlic. Add chicken and toss to coat. Cover and marinate in the refrigerator at least 8 hours or overnight.

3. Cook the noodles according to the instructions on the package; rinse in a colander under cold running water, drain and set aside.

4. Remove the chicken from the marinade and drain well, reserving the marinade. Spread the cornstarch (cornflour) on a plate and toss with the chicken to coat the chicken.

5. Heat the oil in a wok or skillet until smoking, then add the chicken and cook, stirring, until browned all over. Add the honey and heat through. Pour in the reserved marinade and cook, stirring to loosen browned bits from the bottom of the skillet. Simmer, stirring frequently, for about 3–4 minutes or until the chicken is cooked.

6. Season with soy sauce and cayenne pepper and add the orange zest strips.

7. Place the drained noodles on plates or a large platter. Arrange the orange chicken on top and sprinkle with the scallion rings. Serve at once.

BLACKENED INDIAN CHICKEN STICKS ON A BED OF SALAD

Ingredients

For the marinade:

3 tbsp cumin seeds

2 garlic cloves, crushed

Thumb-size piece fresh ginger, peeled and grated

4 tbsp vegetable oil

1 tsp salt

2 tsp garam masala

Juice of half a lemon

½ cup / 125 ml cup yogurt

½ tsp chili powder

4 chicken breasts, skinned

2 tbsp butter

To serve:

Arugula (rocket), cherry tomatoes and pitta breads

Method

Prep and cook time: 30 min plus 2 hours to marinate

1. Toast the cumin seeds in a dry pan for 2 minutes then crush.

2. Mix the cumin seeds with the garlic, ginger, 2 tbsp of the oil, salt, garam masala, lemon juice, yogurt and chili powder.

3. Put the chicken breasts between two sheets of plastic wrap (clingfilm) and bash with a rolling pan to flatten. Slice into strips, mix the chicken with the marinade and set aside for 2 hours.

4. Heat the butter and the remaining oil in a skillet and fry the chicken strips on all sides, basting with the marinade, until browned and cooked through.

5. Serve with the arugula (rocket), cherry tomatoes and pitta breads.

CHICKEN TIKKA MASALA

Ingredients

1 oven-ready chicken, 2½–3 lb /
1.2–1.4 kg

1 lemon

Salt & freshly milled pepper

For the marinade:

2 tsp freshly grated ginger

2 cloves garlic, crushed

2 cups / 500 g yogurt

2 tbsp vegetable oil

2 tbsp paprika

Spice mixture: ½ tsp each of ground
cumin, black pepper, chili powder
and curcuma (turmeric)

1 tbsp chopped cilantro (coriander)
leaves

Method

Prep and cook time: 1 hour 15 min plus
8 hours to marinate

1. Joint the chicken into 6–8 pieces. Score
the surface of the chicken pieces to a depth
of ¼ inch (5 mm) and put into a shallow
dish. Sprinkle with pepper, salt and the juice
of a lemon. Let stand for about 30 minutes.

2. Mix all the spices for the marinade with
the yogurt and oil. Coat the chicken pieces
generously with the marinade and seal
the dish with aluminum foil. Marinate the
chicken in the refrigerator for 8 hours
or overnight.

3. Preheat the oven to 350°F (180°C /
Gas Mark 4). Line a cookie sheet with
aluminum foil and put the chicken pieces
on the sheet. Reserve the marinade. Cook
the chicken in the oven for 35–40 minutes,
brushing frequently with marinade (using
about a quarter), and adding a little water if
necessary.

4. Heat the remaining marinade in a large
pan and add the chicken pieces. Continue to
heat very gently for 5 minutes, then sprinkle
with cilantro (coriander) and serve with rice.

CHICKEN PAD THAI

Ingredients

8 oz / 225 g rice noodles

2 boneless chicken breasts, skinned

2 tbsp soy sauce

2–3 tbsp oyster sauce

1 onion

3 garlic cloves

1 red chili

2 scallions (spring onions)

1 lime

5 oz / 150 g unsalted cashew nuts

3 tbsp vegetable oil

Salt and pepper

8 oz / 225 g peeled shrimps (prawns)

2/3 cup / 150 ml chicken broth (stock)

4 sprigs fresh cilantro (coriander),
to garnish

Method

Prep and cook time: 45 min

1 Cook the noodles according to the packet instructions. Rinse under cold water and drain well.

2 Meanwhile, slice the chicken breasts into strips. Put in a large bowl, add the soy and oyster sauces and leave to marinate for a few minutes.

3 Chop the onion and finely chop the garlic. Finely chop the chili, discarding the seeds. Finely chop the white parts of the scallions (spring onions) and slice the green parts on the diagonal into rings. Cut the lime into 8 wedges. Roughly chop the cashew nuts.

4 Heat the oil in a wok. Add the chicken slices, reserving the marinade, and sear quickly. Remove from the wok and season with salt.

5 Add the onions, garlic and chili to the remaining oil in the wok. Add the shrimps (prawns) and fry briefly. Pour in the broth (stock) and simmer for 2 minutes.

6 Mix the noodles, chicken and reserved marinade together. Season with salt and pepper. Add the scallions and mix together. Turn the mixture into the wok and heat through, ensuring the chicken is thoroughly cooked.

7 Serve sprinkled with the cashew nuts, garnished with cilantro (coriander) sprigs and accompanied with the lime wedges.

CHICKEN AND CASHEW STIR-FRY

Ingredients

4 tbsp sesame oil

4 chicken breasts, skinned and cut into chunks

2 tbsp cornstarch (cornflour)

1 green chili pepper, deseeded and chopped

1 green bell pepper, deseeded and chopped

3 scallions (spring onions), sliced

8 canned water chestnuts, sliced

½ cup / 75 g cashew nuts

4 tbsp oyster sauce

Juice of 1 lime

2–3 tbsp light soy sauce

Method

Prep and cook time: 25 min

1. Heat the oil in a wok or deep skillet until smoking. Dust the chicken pieces with the cornstarch and stir fry them for 3–4 minutes or until slightly crispy. Remove the chicken from the wok.

2. Add a little more oil to the wok and fry the chili pepper for 1 minute. Add the bell pepper and scallions and cook for 2 more minutes.

3. Return the chicken to the wok with the water chestnuts and cashew nuts. Stir in the oyster sauce, lime juice and soy sauce and serve immediately with rice.

CHICKEN KEBABS WITH RAITA

Ingredients

For the kebabs:

1 garlic clove, finely chopped

2 tsp curcuma (turmeric)

1 tsp curry powder

2 tbsp oil

Juice of ½ lime

4 chicken breasts, skinned and cut into chunks

For the raita:

1 cup / 250 ml yogurt

½ cucumber, deseeded and chopped

2 mint sprigs, leaves chopped

1 green chili pepper, chopped

1 tsp salt

Lime wedges, to garnish

Method

Prep and cook time: 20 min plus 2 hours marinating time

1. Mix together the garlic, curcuma (turmeric), curry powder, oil and lime juice. Mix in the chicken chunks and leave to marinate for 2 hours.

2. For the raita, mix togther all the ingredients and set aside.

3. Heat the broiler (grill) to a medium setting. Thread the chicken onto wooden skewers and broil (grill) for about 6 minutes, turning from time to time, or until the chicken is cooked through.

4. Serve the kebabs with the raita and garnish with lime wedges.

DUCK BREAST WITH CELERY

Ingredients

1 tbsp hoisin sauce

2 tbsp rice wine or dry sherry

1 tsp orange juice

½ tsp cornstarch (cornflour)

1 lb / 450 g skinless boneless duck breasts, sliced into matchsticks

2 tbsp vegetable oil

2 garlic cloves, minced

5 celery stalks, cut into matchsticks

2 scallions (spring onions), thinly sliced

1 red bell pepper, sliced into thin strips

Method

Prep and cook time: 15 min plus
1 hour to marinate

1. In a medium bowl, mix the hoisin sauce, rice wine or sherry, the orange juice and cornstarch (cornflour). Add the duck and toss to coat well. Cover and chill for 1 hour.

2. Heat the oil in a wok or large skillet and stir-fry the garlic for 1 minute.

3. Add the duck and stir-fry, keeping the heat high, until cooked through, about 5 minutes.

4. Add the celery, scallions (spring onions) and bell pepper and stir-fry for 2 more minutes, until the vegetables are softened. Serve at once.

BUTTER CHICKEN

Ingredients

½ cup / 125 ml yogurt

3 tbsp ground almonds

2–3 tsp garam masala

1 pinch Indian five-spice powder

1 pinch cinnamon

1 cardamom pod, crushed

1 tsp ground ginger

2 garlic cloves, crushed

1 cup / 200 g canned tomatoes, chopped

1 tsp salt

4 medium chicken breasts, skinned and chopped into bite-size chunks

3 tbsp clarified butter or oil

1 onion, finely chopped

½ cup / 125 ml coconut milk

½ cup / 125 ml vegetable broth (stock) or water

2 handfuls spinach, washed

Salt and pepper

Method

Prep and cook time: 40 min plus 3 hours to marinate

1. Mix the yogurt, ground almonds, garam masala, five-spice, cinnamon, cardamom, ginger, garlic, tomatoes and salt.

2. Put the chicken into a large bowl and pour the yogurt sauce over it. Mix and leave to stand in a cool place for at least 3 hours.

3. Heat the butter in a deep skillet, add the onions and cook for 5 minutes.

4. Add the chicken and yogurt mixture, coconut milk and vegetable broth (stock). Bring to a boil then simmer over a low heat for 20 minutes or until the chicken is cooked through and the sauce has thickened.

5. Stir in the spinach and cook very gently for 5 minutes. Season to taste with salt and serve.

KUNG PAO

Ingredients

3 tbsp vegetable oil

4 skinless boneless chicken breasts, cut into cubes

3 red chili peppers, seeded and sliced into thin strips

3 garlic cloves, roughly chopped

2 scallions (spring onions), finely chopped

½ cup / 75 g peanuts

1 tsp sugar

2 tbsp rice wine

Soy sauce, to taste

Method

Prep and cook time: 20 min

1. In a large skillet or wok, heat the vegetable oil until very hot. Add the chicken and chilies and stir-fry until the chicken is seared, 2–3 minutes.

2. Add the garlic, scallions (spring onions), peanuts and sugar and continue frying for 1–2 minutes.

3. Add the rice wine and a little water, if needed, and simmer for 1–2 minutes, until cooked. Season with soy sauce and serve at once.

ROAST DUCK BREAST WITH VEGETABLES

Ingredients

4 tbsp vegetable oil

4 duck breasts

1 green chili pepper, deseeded and very finely chopped

1 scallion (spring onion), very finely chopped

1 clove garlic, very finely chopped

Thumb-size piece fresh ginger, peeled and finely chopped

4 tbsp light soy sauce

3 tbsp rice vinegar

1 tbsp sugar

3 tbsp sesame oil

For the vegetables:

2 tbsp vegetable oil

4 scallions (spring onions), green parts only; finely shredded

6 iceberg lettuce leaves

Method

Prep and cook time: 30 min

1. Heat the oven to 400°F (200°C / Gas Mark 6).

2. Heat the vegetable oil in an ovenproof skillet over a high heat and cook the duck breasts skin side down for 5 minutes. Turn them over and transfer the pan to the oven. Roast for 15–20 minutes then set aside to rest in a warm place.

3. Meanwhile, mix together the chili, scallion (spring onion), garlic, ginger, soy sauce, vinegar, sugar and sesame oil and set aside.

4. For the vegetables, heat the oil in a wok over a very high heat and add the scallions. Fry until crispy then stir in the iceberg lettuce. Remove the wok from the heat.

5. Slice the duck breasts and serve on a bed of the vegetables with the sauce alongside.

CHICKEN WITH CHILIES AND BASIL

Ingredients

4 chicken breasts

2 shallots

2 chilies

1 tbsp sesame oil

Light soy sauce

Fish sauce

½ bunch Thai basil, for garnish

Method

Prep and cook time: 30 min

1. Cut the chicken into bite-size pieces.

2. Halve and deseed the chilies and cut into very thin strips. Peel and halve the shallots and slice lengthwise.

3. Heat the oil and brown the meat on all sides. Add the shallots and sauté until translucent.

4. Add the chilies and soy sauce and fish sauce to taste, then cook over a very low heat until the meat is done. Finally mix in the basil leaves and serve in bowls.

CHICKEN WITH SPINACH AND ZUCCHINI

Ingredients

2 tbsp sesame oil

2 chicken breasts, cut into strips

6 oz / 150 g tofu, sliced

2 zucchini (courgettes), sliced thinly lengthwise

2 cups / 150 g button mushrooms, thinly sliced

2 handfuls baby spinach

2 tbsp light soy sauce

Method

Prep and cook time: 30 min

1. Heat the oil in a wok or skillet until smoking and stir fry the strips of chicken breasts for 2 minutes.

3. Add the tofu, zucchini (courgettes) and mushrooms and cook for 3 minutes or until the vegetables are just tender and the chicken is cooked through.

4. Add the baby spinach and cook until it wilts, then splash in the soy sauce.

5. Arrange the chicken, tofu, zucchini, mushrooms and spinach on a bed of rice.

CHICKEN WITH RED PEPPERS

Ingredients

4 tbsp soy sauce

2 tbsp sherry

Thumb-size piece ginger, peeled and grated

4 chicken breasts, peeled and chopped into cubes

3 tbsp vegetable oil

2 garlic cloves, crushed

4 shallots, cut into wedges

2 red bell peppers, deseeded and cut into chunks

1 cup / 150 g cashew nuts

2 tbsp hoisin sauce

Method

Prep and cook time: 30 min plus
1 hour to marinate

1. Mix 2 tbsp of the soy sauce with the sherry and ginger and rub into the chicken pieces. Set aside to marinade for 1 hour.

2. Heat the vegetable oil in a wok until just smoking. Add the garlic, shallots, chicken and bell peppers and stir fry for about 5 minutes or until the chicken is cooked through.

3. Add the cashew nuts, hoisin sauce and remaining soy sauce and fry briefly. Serve immediately on a bed of rice.

CHICKEN WITH GINGER-COCONUT SAUCE

Ingredients

8 chicken legs

3 tbsp oil

1 tsp spice mixture, (equal parts of ground ginger, black and white pepper, cayenne pepper)

3 shallots, finely diced

2 garlic cloves, finely chopped

1 tsp ginger, freshly grated

2 chilies, finely chopped

2/3 cup / 150 ml white wine

1 cup / 240 ml coconut milk

1 tbsp honey

8 oz / 225 g tub of crème fraîche

Salt & freshly milled pepper

1 tbsp fish sauce

2 tbsp cilantro (coriander), chopped

Kebab skewers

Method

Prep and cook time: 40 min

1. Skin the chicken legs, take the meat off the bone and dice.

2. Mix 2 tablespoons of oil with the spice mixture and mix with the chicken. Cover and chill.

3. Meanwhile, heat the rest of the oil and sauté the shallots and garlic without browning. Stir in the ginger and chili, then add the white wine.

4. Boil until reduced, then add the coconut milk, honey and crème fraîche and simmer, stirring occasionally, to produce a creamy sauce. Strain through a sieve, add the cilantro (coriander) and add seasoning and fish sauce to taste.

5. Thread the chicken onto skewers and fry or grill for about 5–6 minutes, turning frequently, until cooked. Put on plates and pour the sauce over.

RED CHICKEN CURRY

Ingredients

For the red curry paste:

About 1 inch / 2.5 cm galangal

1 shallot, peeled

1 clove garlic, peeled

About 1 inch / 2.5 cm lemongrass

2 Thai chilies

Zest of a kaffir lime, plus some leaves for garnish

½–1 tsp shrimp paste

Salt

1 lb 6 oz / 600 g chicken breasts

3 tomatoes

1 cup / 200 g pineapple pieces

2 stalks lemongrass

1 tbsp oil

1¾ cups / 400 ml unsweetened coconut milk

1 tbsp brown sugar

3 tbsp fish sauce

2 tbsp lime juice

Method

Prep and cook time: 30 min

1. For the red curry paste place all the ingredients except for the shrimp paste and the salt in a mortar and finely crush. Now mix in the salt and the shrimp paste and stir until smooth.

2. Cut the chicken breasts into 1 inch (2.5 cm) pieces. Place the tomatoes into boiling water, then immediately into cold water. Peel, quarter, de-seed and chop the tomatoes. Chop the pineapple into small pieces. Trim the lemongrass, then finely chop.

3. Heat the oil in a wok or skillet. Fry the curry paste, then pour in the coconut milk and bring to a boil. Season with lemongrass, sugar, fish sauce and lime juice. Add the chicken pieces and the pineapple and simmer for about 5 minutes. Now add the tomatoes and heat until the chicken is cooked.

4. Divide into 4 bowls and serve.

DUCK WITH BOK CHOY

Ingredients

4 tbsp sesame oil, divided

1 clove garlic, minced

1 chili pepper, seeded and chopped

1 inch / 3-cm piece fresh ginger root, minced

2 boneless duck breasts, each around 12 oz / 350 g

Salt and freshly ground pepper

1 red bell pepper, seeded and roughly chopped

1 yellow bell pepper, seeded and roughly chopped

4 scallions (spring onions), sliced into rings

1 lb 8 oz / 600 g bok choy, white parts chopped and green parts thinly sliced

2 tbsp soy sauce, plus more to taste

1 tbsp sesame paste

1 tsp honey

1 tsp rice vinegar

Method

Prep and cook time: 1 hour plus 1 hour to marinate

1. In a medium bowl, combine 2 tbsp of the sesame oil with the garlic, chili pepper and ginger to make a marinade. Add the duck breasts and toss to coat. Cover and marinate in the refrigerator 1 hour.

2. Preheat the oven to 250°F (120°C / Gas Mark 1).

3. Place the duck breasts skin side down in a skillet and fry over medium heat for 6 to 8 minutes until golden brown. Turn over and cook for a further minute, then season with salt and pepper.

4. Place the duck breasts on a wire rack in a roasting pan in the oven and roast for 20–25 minutes.

5. Meanwhile, return the skillet to the heat and add the remaining 2 tbsp sesame oil. Add the red and yellow bell peppers and scallions (spring onions) and stir-fry until softened. Add the bok choy and continue frying for 2–3 minutes.

6. Add 2 tbsp soy sauce, the sesame paste, honey and rice vinegar and bring to a boil. Season to taste with soy sauce, salt and pepper.

7. Remove the duck from the oven, and chop into bite-size pieces. Toss with the vegetables and serve at once.

CHICKEN WITH OYSTER SAUCE AND NOODLES

Ingredients

1 lb / 450 g udon noodles

1 lb 8 oz/ 650 g skinless boneless chicken breasts, chopped into bite-size pieces

Salt and pepper

5 tbsp sesame oil, divided

4-inch / 10-cm piece lemongrass

1 garlic clove, minced

1 scallion (spring onion), finely chopped

3 tbsp oyster sauce

2 tbsp light soy sauce

1 tsp sugar

Method

Prep and cook time: 25 min plus 30 min to marinate

1. Cook the noodles in boiling salted water according to package instructions; drain and set aside.

2. In a small bowl, mix the chicken with salt, pepper, lemongrass and 2 tbsp of the sesame oil; marinate for 30 minutes.

3. Heat the remaining 3 tbsp oil in a wok or large skillet and stir-fry the garlic and the scallion (spring onion) for 30 seconds. Add the chicken and fry all together for 3–4 minutes, until the chicken is cooked through. Season with oyster sauce, soy sauce and sugar; discard the lemongrass stalk.

4. Toss the noodles with the chicken and the sauce and heat through; serve at once.

CHICKEN IN TEMPURA BATTER

Ingredients

1 cup / 100 g all purpose (plain) flour

1 tsp baking powder

1 egg white, lightly beaten

1 scallion (spring onion), very finely chopped

Approx 1 cup / 250 ml sparkling mineral water, chilled

2 cups / 500 ml vegetable oil

½ red bell pepper, deseeded and finely diced

½ green bell pepper, deseeded and finely diced

½ yellow bell pepper, deseeded and finely diced

4 chicken breasts, skinned and cut into chunks

3 tbsp cornstarch (cornflour)

Soy sauce for dipping

Method

Prep and cook time: 30 min

1. Beat the flour with the baking powder, egg white, scallion (spring onion) and enough sparkling water to make a batter. Set aside.

2. Heat about 3 tbsp of the oil in a wok or large skillet and cook the diced bell peppers for 2 minutes. Remove from the pan, drain on kitchen paper and keep warm.

3. Toss the chicken chunks in the cornstarch (cornflour), shaking off any excess.

4. Add the rest of the oil to the wok and heat until smoking.

5. Dip the chicken chunks into the batter and fry in batches until golden brown and the chicken is cooked through.

6. Drain on kitchen paper and serve with the bell peppers scattered over and the soy sauce for dipping.

CHICKEN WITH DATES AND MANGO

Ingredients

2 tbsp oil

1 tbsp garam masala

Salt

1 tbsp honey

Cayenne pepper

8 chicken legs (drumsticks)

1 cup mixed rice / 200 g
(basmati and brown rice)

2½ cups / about 600 ml
chicken broth (stock)

2 shallots

1 mango

¹/₃ cup / 50 g dried dates,
roughly chopped

Curry powder: a good pinch
of ginger, curcuma (turmeric),
cardamom, mace, nutmeg,
cinnamon and cumin, all
ground

1 tbsp chopped parsley

1 tbsp chopped mint

Mint leaves to garnish

Method
Prep and cook time: 45 min

1. Mix the oil with the garam masala, salt, honey and cayenne pepper and brush the chicken with the mixture. Put the chicken under a preheated broiler (grill) for about 30 minutes, turning occasionally, until cooked.

2. Meanwhile put the rice into a pan with the chicken broth (stock) and bring to a boil.

3. Peel and chop the shallots and add to the rice.

4. Peel and halve the mango and remove the pit. Dice the flesh and add to the rice after about 20 minutes. Then add the dates and continue cooking gently for 5–10 minutes more, until done. Season with the curry powder, salt and cayenne pepper. Finally stir in the chopped parsley and mint.

5. Serve the chicken drumsticks in bowls on the rice and garnish with mint.

GREEN CHICKEN CURRY

Ingredients

For the green curry paste:

2 scallions (spring onions), trimmed

2 red chili peppers, deseeded and roughly chopped

2 cloves garlic, peeled

1 walnut-sized piece fresh ginger, peeled and grated

1 tsp coriander seeds, crushed

Salt & freshly milled pepper

1 stalk lemongrass, peeled and finely chopped

1 cup / 20 g Thai basil leaves

1 cup / 20 g cilantro (coriander) leaves

3 tbsp olive oil

1 lime, zest and juice

For the chicken:

4 chicken breasts, cut into bite-size pieces

Oil for frying

1¾ cups / 400 ml unsweetened coconut milk

2 tbsp chopped pistachios

2 kaffir lime leaves

1 red chili peppers, deseeded and thinly sliced

1 cup / 20 g cilantro (fresh coriander) leaves

Method

Prep and cook time: 30 min plus 30 min to marinate

1. Place all ingredients for the green curry paste in a blender and process to a coarse paste.

2. Marinate the chicken for about 30 minutes with some of the curry paste. Remove from the marinade and fry in a hot wok in oil for about 4 minutes.

3. Stir in the remaining curry paste, cook for 2 minutes then pour in the coconut milk.

4. Add the pistachios, the kaffir lime leaves, red chili peppers and cilantro leaves. Bring to a boil, then simmer gently for about 25 minutes. Season to taste with salt and serve with rice.

CHICKEN WINGS IN HOISIN SAUCE

Ingredients

12 chicken wings

Salt and pepper,

1 tbsp honey

1 tbsp hoisin sauce

2 cloves garlic, minced

1 inch / 3 cm piece fresh ginger root, peeled and grated

To garnish:

1 tbsp sesame seeds

4 scallions (spring onions), chopped

1 lemon, cut into wedges

Method

Prep and cook time: 45 min plus 15 min to marinate

1. Pre-heat the oven to 375°F (180°C / Gas Mark 5).

2. Place the chicken wings in an ovenproof dish. Season with salt and pepper.

3. To prepare the sauce, in a small bowl, combine the honey, hoisin sauce, garlic and ginger with 3 tbsp water. Spread over the chicken wings and toss to coat. Let marinate for 15 minutes.

4. Roast the chicken for 30 minutes, brushing occasionally with the marinade, until well browned and cooked through. Serve at once, sprinkled with the sesame seeds and chopped scallions (spring onions) and garnished with lemon wedges.

CHICKEN WITH ALMONDS

Ingredients

3 tbsp clarified butter or oil

1 onion, finely chopped

2 garlic cloves, finely sliced

1 tsp curcuma (turmeric)

4 chicken breasts, skinned and cut into chunks

½ cup / 125 ml chicken broth (stock)

½ cup / 125 ml heavy (double) cream

1/3 cup / 50 g ground almonds

4 pieces cinnamon

2/3 cup / 50 g flaked almonds, lightly toasted

2 tbsp chopped parsley

2 tbsp chopped cilantro (coriander) plus some to garnish

Salt and pepper

1 tsp paprika

Method

Prep and cook time: 30 min

1. Heat the butter in a large pan and gently fry the onion and garlic until soft.

2. Stir in the curcuma (turmeric), cook for 2 minutes then add the chicken and stir briefly. Pour over the chicken broth (stock) and cream and stir in the ground almonds and cinnamon.

3. Simmer very gently, stirring from time to time, for about 20 minutes or until the chicken is cooked through.

4. Stir in the flaked almonds and chopped herbs, season with salt and pepper and serve with the paprika sprinkled over and the cilantro (coriander) to garnish.

CHICKEN TONKATSU IN SOY SAUCE

Ingredients

4 chicken breasts, skinned

4 tbsp all purpose (plain) flour

Salt and pepper

2 eggs, beaten

2 cups / 150 g panko breadcrumbs

1 cup / 250 ml vegetable oil

Soy sauce, to serve

Method

Prep and cook time: 20 min

1. Put the chicken breasts between two sheets of plastic wrap (clingfilm) and bash with a rolling pan to flatten.

2. Season the flour with salt and pepper and place in a shallow bowl.

3. Place the beaten eggs in a shallow bowl and the breadcrumbs onto a plate.

4. Heat the oil in a large skillet over a medium heat.

5. Dip the chicken breasts in the flour, shake off any excess then dip into the egg and then the breadcrumbs.

6. Fry the chicken for 3–4 minutes on each side or until golden brown and cooked through. Drain on kitchen paper, cut into slices and serve hot, dipping in the soy sauce.

CHICKEN KORMA

Ingredients

3 tbsp clarified butter or oil

1 onion, finely chopped

Thumb-size piece ginger, peeled and grated

2 garlic cloves, chopped

2 cloves, crushed

1 dried chili pepper, crushed

2 cardamom pods, crushed

1 tsp ground cumin

4 chicken breasts, skinned and cut into chunks

½ cup / 75 g ground almonds

1 cup / 250 ml chicken broth (stock)

½ cup / 125 ml heavy (double) cream

Salt and pepper

1 tbsp chopped cilantro (coriander) leaves

Method

Prep and cook time: 30 min

1. Heat the clarified butter in a large skillet and gently fry the onion, ginger and garlic until soft.

2. Stir in the crushed cloves, chili, cardamom and cumin and cook for 2 minutes, stirring all the time.

3. Add the chicken, brown the meat on all sides then stir in the almonds, chicken broth (stock) and cream. Simmer very gently for about 20 minutes or until the chicken is cooked through and the sauce is thick and creamy. Season to taste with salt and pepper.

4. Serve the korma with the rice and scatter over the cilantro (coriander).

VIETNAMESE MARINATED CHICKEN

Ingredients

4 tbsp light soy sauce

1 tsp tomato paste (purée)

4 chicken breasts, skinned and cut into bite size chunks

4 tbsp vegetable oil

1 onion, finely sliced

2 tsp sugar

6 scallions (spring onions), sliced

2 tbsp fish sauce

Juice of 1 lime

Salt and pepper

Fish sauce for dipping

Method

Prep and cook time: 20 min plus 30 min to marinate

1. Mix together the soy sauce and tomato paste (purée) and add the chicken. Set aside to marinate for 30 minutes.

2. Heat the oil in a wok or large skillet and fry the onions until they are lightly browned. Stir in the sugar and cook for 2 more minutes.

3. Add the chicken pieces and the marinade. Fry the chicken until it is cooked through then stir in the scallions (spring onions).

4. Stir briefly then pour over the fish sauce and lime juice. Season with salt and pepper and serve with fish sauce for dipping.

TANDOORI CHICKEN WITH RAITA

Ingredients

For the chicken:

4 chicken breasts, skinned

1 tsp each: garam masala, ground cumin, curcuma (turmeric)

2 tsp paprika

2 red chili peppers, deseeded and finely chopped

4 garlic cloves, finely chopped

1 tbsp tomato paste (purée)

Thumb-size piece fresh ginger, peeled and finely chopped

4 tbsp yogurt

1 tsp salt

Juice of 1 lemon

For the raita:

1 cup / 250 ml yogurt

½ cucumber, seeds removed and finely sliced

2 sprigs mint, leaves finely chopped

1 tsp salt

½ green chili pepper, deseeded and finely chopped

To serve: 4 tomatoes, chopped and flat breads

Method

Prep and cook time: 20 min plus 8 hours to marinate

1. Cut the chicken breasts into wide strips and set aside.

2. Mix the remaining ingredients for the chicken together to make a paste and rub into the chicken slices. Cover and refrigerate for 8 hours.

3. For the raita, mix together all the ingredients and set aside.

4. Heat the broiler (grill) or barbecue to a medium setting. Thread the chicken slices onto wooden skewers and broil (grill) for about 3 minutes on each side or until the chicken is cooked through.

5. Serve the skewers with the raita, chopped tomatoes and flat breads alongside.

CHICKEN AND CHICKPEA CURRY

Ingredients

Serves 6

8 boneless, skinless chicken thighs

1 tbsp oil

2 tbsp / 25 g butter

2 onions, finely chopped

4 garlic cloves, crushed

1 red chili, sliced and seeds discarded

1 tsp ground cumin

3 tsp cardamom seeds, crushed

1 tsp ground curcuma (turmeric)

2 tsp garam masala

1 tsp grated fresh ginger

1 tsp salt

2 bay leaves, crushed

1¹/₃ cups / 300 ml chicken
broth (stock)

1 x 14 oz / 400 g can chickpeas

Cilantro (coriander) leaves, to garnish

Method

Prep and cook time: 50 min

1. Preheat the oven to 400F (200C / Gas Mark 6). Cut each thigh into 4 pieces. Heat the oil in a skillet (frying pan) and cook the chicken pieces until browned. Remove from the pan.

2. Add the butter to the pan and when hot add the onions, garlic and chili. Cook until just beginning to color, then add the spices and salt. Cook for 1 minute. Add the bay leaves and broth (stock) and bring to the boil. Stir in the chickpeas.

3. Place the chicken in a baking dish and pour over the onion mixture. Cook in the oven for about 30 minutes until the stew is bubbling and the chicken is thoroughly cooked.

4. Serve garnished with cilantro (coriander) leaves.

TURKEY WITH COCONUT SAUCE

Ingredients

1 lb 2 oz / 500 g turkey breast fillets

3 tbsp sesame oil

2 garlic cloves, diced

1 onion, diced

2 tsp freshly grated ginger

1 red chili, deseeded and shredded

Juice and zest of ½ a lime

3¼ cups / 800 ml coconut milk

1⅓ cup / 200 g frozen peas

Salt

Brown sugar

Soy sauce

Cilantro (coriander) leaves,
to garnish

Method

Prep and cook time: 30 min

1. Slice the turkey into short, narrow strips.

2. Heat 2 tablespoons of sesame oil in a wok or a large skillet. Add the garlic, diced onion, grated ginger, chili and lime peel and sauté briefly.

3. Add the coconut milk and cook for about 10 minutes over a low heat until reduced slightly. Add the frozen peas after about 5 minutes. At the end of the 10 minutes add the turkey and cook very gently in the sauce for a few minutes until the meat is done. Add salt, sugar, lime juice and soy sauce to taste.

4. Serve the turkey with rice and garnish with cilantro (coriander).

CHICKEN KERALA

Ingredients

6 tbsp oil

2 red onions, finely sliced

16 curry leaves

1 white onion, finely chopped

2 garlic cloves, chopped

Thumb-size piece ginger, peeled and finely chopped

1 tsp curcuma (turmeric)

1 tsp garam masala

2 red chili peppers, deseeded and finely chopped

1 tsp mustard seeds, crushed

1 tsp coriander seeds, crushed

4 cloves, crushed

1 tsp peppercorns, crushed

1 tsp salt

4 chicken breasts, skinned and cut into chunks

½ cup / 125 ml chicken broth (stock)

½ cup / 125 ml coconut milk

Method

Prep and cook time: 45 min

1. Heat the oil in a large skillet and gently fry the red onions until crisp but not burnt. Remove from the skillet and set aside.

2. Fry the curry leaves for 2 minutes then set aside.

3. Fry the white onion gently until soft but not brown then add the garlic, ginger, curcuma (turmeric), garam masala, chili peppers, mustard seeds, coriander seeds, cloves, peppercorns and salt.

4. Fry the mixture for 2 minutes then add the chicken. Stir briefly then pour in the chicken broth (stock) and coconut milk. Simmer gently, stirring from time to time, for 20 minutes or until the chicken is cooked through.

5. Serve with the fried red onions scattered over and the curry leaves to garnish.

SESAME CHICKEN WITH CASHEWS AND VEGETABLES

Ingredients

1 egg white

2 tsp cornstarch (cornflour)

½ tsp salt

4 skinless boneless chicken breasts

2 tbsp vegetable oil, divided

1 tbsp black sesame seeds

2 tsp dark soy sauce

2 tsp cider vinegar

2 tsp chili bean sauce

1 tbsp sesame oil

2 tsp sugar

1 tbsp rice wine or dry sherry

4 scallions (spring onions), roughly chopped

1 red bell pepper, sliced

1 cup / 200 g baby corn, cut into bite-size pieces

4 tbsp cashew nuts

Method

Prep and cook time: 45 min

1. In a medium bowl, whisk together the egg white, cornstarch and salt. Add the chicken and stir to coat. Refrigerate for 15 minutes.

2. Meanwhile, to prepare the sauce, heat 1 tbsp of the vegetable oil in a small skillet. Add the sesame seeds and stir-fry for 30 seconds until fragrant. Stir in the soy sauce, cider vinegar, chili bean sauce, sesame oil, sugar and rice wine or dry sherry. Bring to a boil, then remove from the heat and set aside.

3. Bring 1½ cups / 350 ml water to a boil in a large skillet or wok. Add the chicken, reduce the heat and simmer until cooked through,

about 4 minutes. Drain, discarding the water. Add the cooked chicken to the sauce and warm through.

4. Return the skillet to the heat and add the remaining tablespoon of vegetable oil. Add the scallions (spring onion), red bell pepper, corn and cashews and stir-fry until the vegetables are softened, 3–5 minutes.

5. Divide the vegetable mixture into 4 bowls. Cut each chicken breast into 5 slices and arrange on top of the vegetables. Drizzle with the sesame sauce and serve at once.

CHICKEN CURRY WITH TOMATOES

Ingredients

3–4 chicken breast fillets
(1 lb 6 oz / 600 g)

2 tbsp sesame oil

2 garlic cloves, chopped

1 tsp freshly chopped ginger

Scant 1 cup / 200 ml unsweetened
coconut milk

1 tbsp tomato paste (purée)

2 tsp red curry paste

Scant ½ cup / 100 ml vegetable
broth (stock)

1 lb 2 oz / 500 g tomatoes

2 sprigs Thai basil

2 sprigs cilantro (coriander)

Salt & freshly milled pepper

Juice of ½ lemon

Method

Prep and cook time: 30 min

1. Cut the chicken breast fillets into strips
approximately ½–¾ inches (1.5–2 cm) wide.

2. Heat the sesame oil in a wok or skillet
and fry the chicken, garlic and ginger for
3–4 minutes.

3. Then stir in the coconut milk, tomato
paste (purée), curry paste and vegetable
broth (stock) and simmer for a further
5 minutes or so.

4. Drop the tomatoes into boiling water for
a few seconds, refresh in cold water, then
skin, quarter, deseed and cut into wedges.
Add to the chicken curry shortly before the
end of cooking time.

5. To serve, roughly chop the basil and
cilantro (coriander) leaves and stir into the
curry. Season with salt and pepper and
add lemon juice to taste. Serve in bowls
accompanied by rice.

TERIYAKI CHICKEN

Ingredients

3 tbsp honey

6 tbsp teriyaki sauce

2 tbsp vegetable oil

1 chicken, trussed

For the salad:

4 oz / 100 g snow peas (mangetout)

2 tbsp rice vinegar

1 tbsp lemon juice

3 tbsp sesame oil

½ tsp salt

2 carrots, peeled and finely sliced lengthways

½ cucumber, peeled and finely sliced lengthways

1 cup / 100 g soya bean sprouts

Method

Prep and cook time: 2 hours plus 2 hours to marinate

1. Mix the honey with the teriyaki sauce and oil and brush the chicken with the mixture. Marinate for 2 hours.

2. Heat the oven to 400F, (200C / Gas Mark 6). Place the chicken on a rack in a roasting pan and roast for 20 minutes.

3. Turn the oven down to 375F (180C / Gas Mark 5), baste the chicken with the marinade and roast for a further 1 hour or until the chicken is cooked through, basting every 20 minutes.

4. Remove the chicken from the oven and rest for 15 minutes.

5. Blanch the snow peas (mangetout) in boiling water for 2 minutes. Drain, refresh in cold water and pat dry with kitchen paper.

6. Mix together the rice vinegar, lemon juice, sesame oil and salt and toss into the salad vegetables and snow peas.

7. Serve the chicken with the salad.

CHICKEN CHOW MEIN

Ingredients

For the noodles:

8 oz / 225 g dried egg noodles

1 tbsp sesame oil

For the chicken and marinade:

2 tsp light soy sauce

2 tsp rice wine or dry sherry

1 tsp sesame oil

½ tsp salt

½ tsp freshly ground white pepper

4 oz / 100 g skinless boneless chicken breast, cut into matchsticks

For the stir-fry:

3 tbsp vegetable oil, divided

1 tbsp minced garlic

½ cup / 50 g snow peas or sugar snap peas, thinly sliced lengthwise

⅓ cup / 50 g shredded cooked ham

2 tsp light soy sauce

2 tsp dark soy sauce

1 tbsp rice wine or dry sherry

1 tsp salt

½ tsp freshly ground pepper

½ tsp sugar

3 tbsp scallions (spring onions), chopped

1 tsp sesame oil

Method
Prep and cook time: 40 min

1. Cook the noodles in a large pot of boiling water for 3–5 minutes, then drain and refresh in cold water. Toss with the sesame oil and set aside.

2. Combine the soy sauce, rice wine or sherry, sesame oil, salt and white pepper in a medium bowl; add the chicken and toss to coat. Let stand 10 minutes to marinate.

3. Heat a skillet or wok over high heat. Add 1 tablespoon of the vegetable oil and when very hot and slightly smoking, add the shredded chicken. Stir-fry for about 2 minutes, then transfer to a plate.

4. Return the wok to the heat, then add the remaining 2 tablespoons vegetable oil. When slightly smoking, add the garlic and stir-fry for 10 seconds. Then add the snow peas or sugar snaps and ham and stir-fry for about 1 minute.

5. Add the chicken with its juices and the light and dark soy sauce; stir-fry for 3–4 minutes until chicken is nearly cooked. Add the rice wine or sherry, salt, pepper, sugar and scallions. Stir-fry for 2 minutes.

6. Add the noodles and sesame oil and give the mixture a few final stirs to reheat. Turn onto a warm platter and serve at once.

SICHUAN BEEF

Ingredients

1 lb / 450 g rump or round steak, thinly sliced

Salt and black pepper

3 tbsp rice wine or dry sherry

2 tbsp vegetable oil

1 onion, chopped

2 cloves garlic, minced

1 inch / 3 cm piece fresh ginger root, peeled and grated

2 large carrots, cut into matchsticks

8-oz / 250 g head of broccoli, stalks peeled and cut into small florets

2 tbsp oyster sauce

Method

Prep and cook time: 25 min

1. In a medium bowl, season the steak with salt and pepper and toss together with the wine or sherry. Cover and leave to marinate for 5 minutes.

2. Heat the oil in a large wok or skillet; add onion and stir-fry until translucent, a few minutes. Add the garlic, ginger and carrots and continue cooking for 2 minutes until softened slightly.

3. Stir in the beef and its juices, the wine or sherry, and broccoli; stir-fry for 3–5 minutes, until the meat is browned and the broccoli is tender-crisp.

4. Pour over the oyster sauce and cook, stirring to coat, 1–2 minutes more, until heated through. Serve immediately.

BEEF BIRYANI WITH FRIED ONIONS

Ingredients

½ cup /125 ml clarified butter or oil

2 onions, finely sliced

2 onions, roughly chopped

2 thumb-size pieces ginger, peeled and roughly chopped

3 garlic cloves, roughly chopped

2 green chili peppers, deseeded and roughly chopped

4 cloves

4 cardamom pods

1 tsp garam masala

1 tsp ground cinnamon

Juice of 2 limes

2 lb / 900 g beef, cut into large chunks

1 cup / 200 g long grain rice

6 strands saffron

Salt and pepper

Mint leaves, to garnish

Method

Prep and cook time: 1 hour 20 min plus 1 hour marinating

1. Put the chopped onions, ginger, garlic, chili peppers, cloves, cardamom pods, cinnamon and lime juice in a food processor and blend briefly to make a coarse purée.

2. Rub the onion purée into the beef and set aside to marinate for 1 hour.

3. Heat the butter in a deep pan and fry the sliced onions until brown and crisp. Remove from the pan, drain on kitchen paper and set aside.

4. Heat the pan with the butter used to cook the sliced onions and add the beef and the marinade. Fry until the meat is browned on all sides then add about 1 cup of water, salt and pepper and simmer very, very gently with a lid on for about 1 hour or until the meat is very tender. Add a little more water during the cooking if needed to prevent the dish burning.

5. While the meat is cooking, prepare the rice according to the packet instructions. Dissolve the saffron strands in a little hot water and stir into half the rice. Mix the saffron rice into the white rice.

6. Serve the meat and its sauce with the rice, scatter over the fried onions and garnish with mint leaves.

PAD THAI WITH BEEF

Ingredients

8 oz / 225 g dried rice noodles

2 tbsp oil

3 garlic cloves, chopped

2 tsp chopped red chilies

14 oz / 400 g beef, for pan-frying,
cut into thin strips

2 tbsp fish sauce

2 tbsp lime juice

2 tsp brown sugar

$^1/_3$ cup / 40 g soybean sprouts

¼ cup / 40 g frozen peas

¼ cup / 40 g canned soybeans, drained

Green scallion (spring onion) stalks,
to garnish

Method

Prep and cook time: 30 min

1. Soak the noodles in warm water for
10 minutes, then drain and set aside.

2. Heat the oil in a wok or a large skillet.
Add the garlic, chilies and beef and stir-
fry for about 4 minutes. Add the drained
noodles, cover and fry for a further minute.

3. Add the fish sauce, lime juice and sugar
and stir well until everything is heated
evenly. Add the soybean sprouts, peas and
soybeans and cook until done.

4. Check the seasoning and serve garnished
with the green stalks of scallion (spring
onion) cut into rings at an angle.

BEEF VINDALOO

Ingredients

3 tbsp clarified butter or oil

1 lb / 450 g braising beef, cut into chunks

2 onions, finely chopped

2 garlic cloves, chopped

2 red chili peppers, deseeded and chopped

1 tsp each of: cumin seeds, mustard seeds, curcuma (turmeric) and paprika

2 tsp ground coriander

2 tsp garam masala

½ tsp dried chili flakes (optional)

2 tbsp tomato paste (purée)

2 cups / 400 g canned tomatoes, chopped

⅓ cup / 75 ml white wine vinegar

2 cups / 500 ml beef broth (stock)

Salt and pepper

Mint leaves, to garnish

Poppadoms, to serve

Method

Prep and cook time: 1 hour 15 min

1. Heat the butter in a large pan and gently fry the pieces of meat in batches until they are brown all over. Remove from the pan and set aside.

2. Fry the onions in the pan until soft but not brown then add the garlic, chili peppers and all the spices. Cook for 2 minutes then stir in the tomato paste (purée).

3. Return the meat to the pan, cook for about a minute then add the canned tomatoes, vinegar and beef broth (stock). Season with salt and pepper and simmer very gently for about 45 minutes or until the meat is very tender.

4. Serve the curry garnished with mint leaves and poppadoms alongside.

DAN DAN NOODLES

Ingredients

For the meat topping:

1 tbsp vegetable oil

3 dried chilies, halved
(discard seeds)

½ tsp whole Sichuan
peppercorns

2 tbsp / 25 g Sichuan ya cai
or preserved mustard leaves*

4 oz / 100 g ground
(minced) beef

2 tsp light soy sauce

Salt

12 oz / 350 g dried wide
Chinese noodles or fettuccini

For the sauce:

1 tsp ground roasted Sichuan
peppercorns

1 tbsp light soy sauce

1 tbsp dark soy sauce

2 tbsp chili oil

To garnish:

1 scallion (spring onion),
finely chopped

Method
Prep and cook time: 30 min

1. For the meat topping, heat the oil in a wok
or skillet over a medium heat. Add the chilies
and Sichuan peppercorns and stir-fry for
30 seconds. Add the ya cai or preserved
mustard leaves and continue to stir-fry for
2 minutes.

2. Add the beef and cook, stirring, for
10 minutes until the meat is browned all over.
Splash in the soy sauce and stir-fry until the meat
is a little crisp. Season with salt and keep warm.

3. Bring a pot of salted water to a boil. Add
the noodles and cook until tender, 4 minutes.

4. Meanwhile, in a small bowl, combine the
roasted Sichuan peppercorns, light and dark
soy sauce and chili oil to make a sauce.

5. Drain the noodles. Divide the meat
between 4 bowls, top with the noodles and
drizzle the sauce over each. Garnish with the
chopped scallion (spring onion).

*Look for ya cai (preserved vegetable,
usually mustard leaves) in Asian markets.
If unavailable, just omit it from the recipe.

RED BEEF CURRY

Ingredients

3 tbsp oil

1–2 tsp shrimp paste

½ tsp chili flakes

1 tsp ginger, freshly grated

1 onion, finely diced

2 cloves garlic, minced

1 lb 6 oz / 600 g beef, e. g. rump,
cut into strips

1 cup / 250 ml coconut milk

14 oz / 400 g sweet potatoes, peeled
and roughly chopped

2 red bell peppers, deseeded and
cut into strips

1½ cups / 250 g string beans, trimmed

2 kaffir lime leaves

Salt

Light soy sauce

Method

Prep and cook time: 50 min

1. Fry the shrimp paste, chili, ginger, onion
and garlic in hot oil.

2. Add the meat and fry, then pour in the
coconut milk. Add a little water and the
vegetables.

3. Throw in the lime leaves and simmer
gently for about 30 minutes, stirring
occasionally. Add a little water if needed.
Season with salt and soy sauce and serve.

KOFTA CURRY

Ingredients

For the sauce:

3 tbsp oil

1 onion, chopped

2 garlic cloves, chopped

Thumb-size piece ginger, finely chopped

1 tsp each of: curcuma (turmeric), chili powder, paprika, ground cinnamon and ground coriander

2 cups / 400 g canned tomatoes

1 cup / 250 ml vegetable broth (stock)

Salt and pepper

For the kofta:

1 onion, roughly chopped

2 garlic cloves, chopped

2 tbsp chopped cilantro (coriander)

2 tbsp chopped parsley

1 tsp ground cinnamon

1 lb / 450 g ground (minced) beef

1 egg, beaten

4 tbsp oil

For the batter:

4 eggs

50 g / ½ cup flour

1 tsp baking powder

1 tsp salt

Oil, for deep frying

To serve:

12 cherry tomatoes, quartered

Chopped parsley

Method

Prep and cook time: 1 hour

1. For the sauce, heat the oil in a deep pan and gently cook the onion until soft but not brown.

2. Add the garlic, ginger and all the spices and cook for 2 minutes, stirring all the time.

3. Pour in the tomatoes and vegetable broth (stock), season with salt and pepper and simmer gently for 15 minutes.

4. Blend the sauce to a purée, pass through a fine sieve and keep warm.

5. For the koftas, put the onion, garlic, cilantro (coriander) and parsley in a food processor and blend to make a paste.

6. Mix the paste with the beef and beaten egg, season with salt and pepper and roll into balls.

7. Heat the oil in a skillet and fry the koftas for 5 minutes making sure they are evenly cooked.

8. Beat the batter ingredients together with half a cup of warm water. Heat the oil in a deep pan until bubbles appear on a wooden spoon held in the oil. Dip the koftas into the batter and deep fry in batches until golden brown. Drain on kitchen paper.

9. Serve the koftas in the sauce with the cherry tomatoes and parsley scattered over.

BEEF WITH CABBAGE AND MUSHROOMS

Ingredients

2 tbsp vegetable oil

10 oz / 300 g lean beef steak, sliced

½ Napa cabbage (Chinese leaves), sliced

1 red bell pepper, sliced into strips

10 oz / 300 g Asian mushrooms (try straw, oyster, shiitake or enoki), sliced if large

2 tsp cornstarch (cornflour)

2 tsp dry sherry

Scant ½ cup / 100 ml beef broth (stock)

2 tsp dark soy sauce

Enoki mushrooms, to garnish

Method

Prep and cook time: 20 min

1. Heat the oil in a large wok or skillet, add the beef and stir-fry just until browned, 3 minutes. Add the cabbage and bell pepper and stir-fry for 1 minute. Add the mushrooms and cook for 2 minutes more; set aside and keep warm.

2. In a small bowl, mix the cornstarch (conflour) with the sherry to a smooth paste.

3. In a medium saucepan, combine the broth (stock) and soy sauce; stir in the cornstarch mixture. Bring to a boil and cook, stirring, until the sauce is thickened.

4. Add the sauce to the beef and vegetables; heat through and serve at once, garnished with enoki mushrooms.

BEEF CURRY WITH POTATOES AND NUTS

Ingredients

For the curry paste:

1 shallot, peeled

2 cloves garlic, peeled

1 inch / 4 cm galangal

2 red chilies

1 tsp shrimp paste

Salt

1lb 6oz / 600 g beef

2 shallots, finely chopped

2 cloves garlic, finely chopped

3 tbsp sesame oil

2 dried red chilies

½ cup / 50 g peanuts, fresh, not salted

3 cups / 800 ml coconut cream

14 oz/400 g boiling potatoes

4 tbsp fish sauce

1 tbsp oyster sauce

2 tbsp brown sugar

2 tbsp lime juice

4 slices of lime, fried

Method
Prep and cook time: 1 hour 30 min

1. For the curry paste, crush the shallot and garlic with the galangal and chili in a mortar until smooth or process in a blender. Stir in the shrimp paste and salt to taste. Set aside.

2. Cut the beef into thin strips.

3. Heat 1 tablespoon of the oil in a wok and fry the shallots, the garlic and the chilies over a high heat until the shallots are golden brown. Take out of the wok. Let cool slightly, then place in the mortar and crush to a smooth paste.

4. Put the peanuts in the wok and toast until golden brown. Transfer the peanuts to a clean mortar and crush.

5 Fry the meat in the remaining oil over a high heat and pour in half of the coconut cream. Bring to a boil, then reduce the heat and simmer for 45 minutes.

6. In the meantime, peel the potatoes and cut into about 1 inch (3 cm) cubes.

7. Take the meat and the sauce out of the wok and clean the wok. Then sauté the curry paste in the wok, pour in the remaining coconut cream, add the potatoes, the crushed peanuts and the shallot paste and bring to a boil. Cook for 5 minutes, then add the meat and season with fish sauce, oyster sauce and sugar. Simmer for about 25 minutes over a medium heat until the potatoes are cooked.

8. Season to taste with lime juice and spoon into bowls. Garnish with fried lime slices and serve.

GRILLED STEAK WITH VEGETABLES AND WASABI

Ingredients

3 tbsp vegetable oil

4 sirloin steaks

3 tbsp sesame oil

2 carrots, peeled and sliced

1 cup / 100 g button mushrooms, sliced

2 tbsp light soy sauce

1 tbsp rice vinegar

2 tsp wasabi paste

Watercress, to garnish

Method

Prep and cook time: 20 min

1. Heat the vegetable oil in a griddle pan until smoking. Cook the steaks for about 3 minutes on each side, turning once to make a criss-cross pattern. Remove the steaks from the pan, drizzle over the pan juices and set aside in a warm place.

2. Heat the sesame oil in a wok over a high heat and stir fry the carrots and button mushrooms for 3 minutes. Add the soy sauce and vinegar and cook for 1 more minute.

3. Slice the steaks and serve on a bed of rice and vegetables with the a dab of wasabi paste and watercress to garnish.

BEEF WITH BLACK BEANS

Ingredients

3 tbsp toasted sesame oil, divided

8 shallots, quartered

2 inch / 5 cm piece fresh ginger root, peeled and thinly sliced

2 cloves garlic, thinly sliced

1 head broccoli, stems peeled and cut into small florets

2 heads bok choy, quartered lengthwise

12 oz / 300 g rump steak, thinly sliced and threaded onto skewers

Generous ½ cup / 150 g black bean stir-fry sauce

Method

Prep and cook time: 20 min

1 Heat 2 tablespoons of the oil in a large skillet over medium heat. Add the shallots, ginger and garlic and stir-fry for 2 minutes or until just beginning to color.

2. Add the broccoli and bok choy and stir-fry for 2–3 minutes until wilted, but still crisp. Divide between 4 plates or bowls and keep warm.

3. Heat the remaining tablespoon of oil in the skillet over high heat. Add the steak skewers and cook, turning occasionally, for 2 minutes or until well browned and cooked to your liking. Reduce the heat.

4. Pour the black bean sauce over the top and add 5 tablespoons of cold water. Cook, stirring gently for 1 minute until the beef is well coated and the sauce is hot. Spoon over the vegetables and serve immediately.

MAIN DISHES

FISH AND SEAFOOD

SEA BASS STEAKS WITH INDIAN SPICES

Ingredients

2 tbsp clarified butter or oil

2 onions, chopped

1 red chili pepper, deseeded and finely chopped

1 tsp curcuma (turmeric)

1 tbsp garam masala

1 tbsp red curry paste

2 tomatoes, roughly chopped

3 tbsp lime juice, plus extra to taste

½ cup / 125 ml coconut milk

2 cups / 500 ml fish or vegetable broth (stock)

4 sea bass steaks

Cilantro (fresh coriander), chopped

Salt and pepper

Method

Prep and cook time: 45 min

1. Heat the butter in a deep skillet and fry the onions on a medium heat for 3–4 minutes.

2. Add the chili pepper, curcuma (turmeric), garam masala, red curry paste and tomatoes and fry together for 1 minute. Stir in the lime juice, coconut milk and broth (stock). Simmer for 5–8 minutes with a lid on.

3. Add the fish to the sauce and cook on a low heat for 7–10 minutes. The fish is cooked when the flesh comes away from the bone.

4. Just before serving stir the cilantro (coriander) into the sauce. Season with salt, pepper and lime juice.

BRAISED
SICHUAN FISH

Ingredients

1 tbsp sunflower or vegetable oil

1 garlic clove, chopped

7 tbsp / 100 ml fish broth (stock)

2 tbsp fish sauce

2 tbsp soy sauce

1 tsp cornstarch (cornflour), mixed to a smooth paste in 1 tbsp water

1 cup / 100 g bean sprouts, fresh or preserved, rinsed and drained

2 lb / 900 g firm white fish fillets, such as cod, plaice or halibut, chopped into 1-inch / 3 cm strips

6 scallions (spring onions), roughly chopped (reserve a few pieces for garnish)

Salt, to taste

Cayenne pepper, to taste

Method

Prep and cook time: 25 min

1. Heat the oil in a large skillet or wok; add the garlic and cook, stirring, until softened. Add the fish broth (stock), fish sauce and soy sauce and heat through.

2. Stir in the cornstarch (cornflour) mixture. Bring to a boil and cook, stirring, until slightly thickened.

3. Add the bean sprouts, fish and half of the scallions (spring onions), cover and simmer for 4–5 minutes.

4. Season with salt and cayenne pepper and serve scattered with the remaining scallions.

TERIYAKI SALMON WITH EGG NOODLES

Ingredients

2 sheets egg noodles

3 tbsp vegetable oil

2 garlic cloves, finely chopped

Thumb-size piece of fresh ginger, peeled and grated

4 tbsp dark soy sauce

2 tbsp maple syrup

4 salmon fillets, skinned and cut into bite size pieces

2 scallions (spring onions), sliced

1 red bell pepper, deseeded and sliced

8 oz / 200 g snow peas (sugar snaps)

1 tbsp sesame oil

Juice of 1 lime

Method

Prep and cook time: 15 min

1. Cook the noodles according to the packet instructions. Drain.

1. Meanwhile, heat the vegetable oil in a wok or deep skillet over a high heat until smoking.

2. Add the garlic and ginger, cook for 30 seconds then add the soy sauce and maple syrup.

3. Add the salmon pieces, gently stir fry for 2 minutes then add the scallions (spring onion), bell pepper and snow peas (sugar snaps).

4. Stir fry for 2 more minutes then add the sesame oil and lime juice.

5. Stir in the cooked noodles, mix well and serve immediately.

SHRIMP CURRY

Ingredients

1 onion, roughly chopped

2 garlic cloves, chopped

Thumb-size piece ginger, peeled and chopped

1 red chili pepper, deseeded and chopped

3 tbsp clarified butter or oil

1 tsp salt

1 tsp paprika

1 tsp garam masala

½ tsp curcuma (turmeric)

2 tbsp tomato paste (purée)

2 cups / 500 ml coconut milk

1 cup / 250 ml fish broth (stock) or water

1 lb 8 oz / 650 g large shrimps, peeled with tail on

Salt and pepper

Cilantro (coriander) leaves, to garnish

Method

Prep and cook time: 30 min

1. Put the onion, garlic, ginger and chili pepper in a food processor and blend to make a purée.

2. Heat the butter in a wide pan and add the onion mixture. Cook for 1 minute then add the salt, paprika, garam masala and curcuma (turmeric) and cook for 2 minutes, stirring all the time.

3. Stir in the tomato paste (purée) then pour in the coconut milk and fish broth (stock). Bring to a boil then simmer gently for 10 minutes.

4. Add the shrimps, season with salt and pepper and cook for a few minutes. Serve garnished with cilantro (coriander) and accompanied with boiled rice.

TUNA SASHIMI

Ingredients

1 lb / 400 g very fresh tuna

3 tomatoes

½ cucumber, peeled, deseeded and finely chopped

½ red onion, very finely chopped

2 tbsp salmon caviar

2 handfuls mixed oriental salad leaves

2 tbsp sesame oil

Juice of 1 lime

Method

Prep and cook time: 15 min plus 20 mins chilling time

1. Wrap the tuna tightly in plastic wrap (clingfilm) and chill in the freezer for 20 minutes.

2. Drop the tomatoes in boiling water for 30 seconds, drain and peel off the skins. Discard the seeds and finely dice the flesh.

3. Remove the tuna from the freezer and discard the plastic wrap. Slice the tuna thinly with a very sharp knife and arrange on serving plates.

4. Scatter over the tomatoes, cucumber, onion and caviar, top with a pile of salad leaves and drizzle over the sesame oil and lime juice.

STEAMED SALMON WITH GARLIC OIL

Ingredients

4 salmon filets with skin, each around 200 g / 7 oz

Salt and freshly ground pepper, to taste

Juice of 1 lime

4 tbsp light sesame oil

8 cloves garlic, minced

2 scallions (spring onions), chopped into 2 inch / 5 cm strips

Method

Prep and cook time: 20 min

1. Season the salmon with salt and pepper and drizzle with lime juice.

2. In a large skillet or wok, heat the oil, then add the garlic and stir-fry. As soon as the garlic begins to color, remove from the heat and stir in the scallions (spring onions). Set aside.

3. Bring 2 inches / 5 cm of water to a boil in a steamer. Place the salmon in the steamer insert, cover and steam until barely firm in the center, around 7 minutes.

4. To serve, arrange the salmon on plates, and top with the garlic-scallion mixture.

COCONUT FISH CURRY WITH MANGO

Ingredients

2 cloves garlic, chopped

Thumb-size piece of ginger, peeled and chopped

1 red chili pepper, deseeded and chopped

1 stem lemongrass, chopped

Juice of 1 lime

2 tbsp fish sauce

½ tsp sugar

3 tbsp vegetable oil

1½ lb / 650 g white fish fillet, cod, haddock or halibut

Salt and pepper

3½ cups / 800 ml coconut milk

2 mangoes, peeled, stone removed and sliced

Mint leaves, to garnish

Cilantro (coriander) leaves, to garnish

Method

Prep and cook time: 30 min

1. Put the garlic, ginger, chili, lemongrass, lime juice, fish sauce and sugar in a blender and whizz together to make a fine curry paste.

2. Heat the oil in a wide skillet. Season the fish fillets with salt and pepper and gently fry for about 3 minutes on each side or until cooked through. Remove the fish from the skillet and set aside in a warm place.

3. Return the skillet to the heat and add the curry paste. Fry for 2 minutes then add the coconut milk. Bring to a boil and simmer gently for 10 minutes.

4. Place the fish and mango slices in warmed serving bowls, pour over the sauce and garnish with the mint and cilantro (coriander) leaves.

FISH CURRY WITH SHRIMP

Ingredients

1 tsp curcuma (turmeric)

2 tsp curry powder

1 lb / 450 g haddock, cut into bite-size pieces, skin and bones removed

4 tbsp ghee or clarified butter

2 onions, finely diced

4 garlic cloves, finely chopped

2 tsp freshly grated ginger

1 tsp mustard seeds

5 oz / 150 g canned tomatoes

1¾ cups / 400 ml unsweetened coconut milk

½ tsp finely chopped red chili

6 oz / 175 g large shrimp or prawns, peeled and ready to cook

Vegetable broth (stock)

1 tbsp finely chopped cilantro (coriander) leaves

Method

Prep and cook time: 35 min

1. Mix the curcuma (turmeric) and curry powder and rub the fish with about half of the mixture. Reserve the remainder.

2. Heat the ghee or clarified butter in a large skillet and sauté the onions and garlic until translucent. Then add the ginger, the remaining spice mix and mustard seeds and fry briefly. Pour in the tomatoes and coconut milk and simmer for about 10 minutes. Purée the sauce, but not too finely.

3. Add the chopped chili, fish and shrimp (or prawns) and cook gently for about 5 minutes, until done. If the sauce is too thick, add a little vegetable broth (stock).

4. Check the seasoning and serve garnished with cilantro (coriander) leaves.

SHRIMP AND PUMPKIN CURRY

Ingredients

For the green curry paste:

1 shallot, roughly chopped

1 peeled garlic clove

1 tbsp cilantro (coriander) leaves

½ tsp coriander seeds

1 tsp freshly grated ginger

1 green chili, deseeded and roughly chopped

2 tbsp oil

1 bunch scallions (spring onions), cut into rings

2 cloves garlic, roughly chopped

2 tsp freshly chopped ginger

1 lb 6 oz / 600 g pumpkin, deseeded and chopped into ½ inch (1 cm) cubes

1¾ cups / 400 ml unsweetened coconut milk

Juice of ½ lemon

Salt & pepper

11 oz / 300 g shrimp (prawns), thawed if frozen

Method

Prep and cook time: 30 min

1. Put all the ingredients for the curry paste into a mortar and crush to make a paste.

2. Heat the oil and sauté the scallions, ginger, garlic and pumpkin over a high heat for 4–5 minutes. Stir in the coconut milk, curry paste and lemon juice, season with salt and pepper and simmer without a lid over a medium heat for about 5 minutes or until the pumpkin has softened

3. Check the seasoning, add the shrimp (prawns) and briefly return to a boil. When the shrimp are cooked, serve in bowls.

MONKFISH IN BANANA LEAVES

Ingredients

4 large banana leaves

2 tbsp oil

1 onion, roughly chopped

2 green chili peppers, deseeded and roughly chopped

Thumb-size piece ginger, peeled and roughly chopped

1 stick lemongrass, roughly chopped

1 garlic clove, roughly chopped

1 handful cilantro (coriander) leaves

Zest and juice of 2 limes

1 cup / 250 ml coconut milk

1 tsp fish sauce

1 tsp sugar

4 pieces monkfish fillet, approx 8 oz / 225 g each, skin on

1 lime, cut into wedges, to garnish

Method

Prep and cook time: 35 min

1. Heat the oven to 425°F (220°C / Gas Mark 7).

2. Soften the banana leaves by carefully holding over a gas flame then set aside.

3. Put all the ingredients apart from the monkfish into a food processor and pulse to make a coarse paste.

4. Slice the skin away from the flesh of the monkfish, leaving a hinge at one end. Place a piece of fish skin side down on each banana leaf, spoon the paste under the skin and wrap up the banana leaf. Secure with kitchen twine.

5. Place the stuffed banana leaves on a cookie sheet and bake in the oven for 20 minutes. Serve with lime wedges.

NOODLES WITH SHRIMP AND VEGETABLES

Ingredients

1 lb / 450 g Chinese egg noodles

2 tbsp vegetable oil

5 oz / 150 g large shrimp (prawns), peeled, deveined and chopped into bite-size pieces

2 tbsp freshly chopped cilantro (fresh coriander)

1 clove garlic, minced

8 oz / 200 g bok choy, thinly sliced

1 red chili pepper, seeded and sliced into thin strips (wear gloves to prevent irritation)

1 tsp five-spice powder

2 tbsp rice wine or dry sherry

2 tbsp black bean sauce

Soy sauce, to taste

Fish sauce, to taste

Method

Prep and cook time: 30 min

1. Cook the noodles according to package instructions. Rinse in a colander under cold running water; drain and set aside.

2. Heat the oil in a large skillet or wok; add the shrimp and cilantro (coriander) and quickly stir-fry until the shrimp are barely translucent. With a slotted spoon, remove the shrimp from the wok and keep warm.

3. Return the wok to the heat and add the garlic, bok choy, chili, and five-spice powder; stir to heat through. Add the wine or sherry and about 4 tablespoons of water; bring to a boil, scraping up browned bits from the bottom of the pan.

4. Add the bean sauce and simmer for around 1–2 minutes, stirring constantly. Stir in the shrimp and noodles and cook, tossing gently to coat, until heated through. Add the soy sauce and fish sauce and season with salt and pepper.

5. Rest briefly to allow the flavors to mingle, then serve in bowls.

COD CURRY
WITH SPINACH

Ingredients

For the spinach:

3 tbsp oil

1 onion, finely chopped

2 garlic cloves, chopped

2 tsp garam masala

4 large handfuls spinach, washed
and finely chopped

1 tbsp butter

Salt and pepper

For the cod curry:

3 tbsp oil

1 tsp chili powder

1 tsp curcuma (turmeric)

2 tsp garam masala

½ cup / 125 ml coconut milk

½ cup / 125 ml fish broth (stock)

1 lb 8 oz / 650 g cod, cut into chunks

Method

Prep and cook time: 40 min

1. For the spinach, heat the oil in wide pan
and cook the onion until soft but not brown.

2. Add the garlic and garam masala and
cook for 2 minutes then add the spinach
and cook very gently, stirring from time
to time, for 10 minutes. Stir in the butter,
season with salt and pepper. Set aside and
keep warm.

3. For the curry, heat the oil in a wide pan
and fry the chili powder, curcuma (turmeric)
and garam masala for 2 minutes.

4. Pour over the coconut milk and fish
broth (stock), bring to a boil and simmer
for 10 minutes. Season with salt and
pepper, add the cod and cook very gently
for 5 minutes or until the cod is just cooked
through.

5. Serve with boiled rice.

NASI GORENG

Ingredients

1 cup / 200 g long grain rice

4 tbsp vegetable oil

12 oz / 300 g shrimp (prawns), peeled and tails removed

2 shallots, finely chopped

2 tbsp medium hot curry paste

½ red bell pepper, deseeded and finely diced

4 scallions (spring onions), sliced

1 carrot, cut into fine batons

1 cup / 150 g frozen peas, thawed

1 tbsp sesame oil

2 handfuls bean sprouts

Method

Prep and cook time: 30 min

1. Cook the rice according to the packet instructions, drain well and set aside.

2. Heat the oil in wok or large skillet and fry the shrimps (prawns) until cooked through. Remove the shrimps from the wok and set aside.

3. Return the wok to the heat and fry the shallots until brown and crispy. Stir in the curry paste, cook for 2 minutes then add the bell pepper, scallions (spring onions), carrots and peas.

4. Cook for 2 minutes then stir in the sesame oil, bean sprouts, prawns and the cooked rice.

5. Stir well and heat through then serve immediately.

SOLE WITH LIME SAUCE

Ingredients

2 soles, filleted

4 lime leaves

2 garlic cloves, finely sliced

2 red chili peppers, deseeded and sliced

Juice of 2 limes

4 tbsp light soy sauce

2 tbsp fish sauce

1 tsp sugar

8 scallions (spring onions), to garnish

Method

Prep and cook time: 25 min

1. Heat the oven to 400°F (200°C / Gas Mark 6).

2. Lay the sole fillets in a shallow non-metallic ovenproof dish. Scatter the garlic, chili and lime leaves over the fish.

3. Mix together the lime juice, soy sauce, fish sauce, sugar and about ½ cup water and pour over the fish.

4. Cover the dish with aluminum foil and bake in the oven for 10–12 minutes or until the fish is just cooked.

5. Serve in warmed bowls with the scallions (spring onions) to garnish.

MUSSELS WITH CURRY SAUCE

Ingredients

6 lb 12 oz / 3 kg mussels

2 red chilies, deseeded and cut into thin rings

2 tbsp oil

2 onions, cut into rings

4 cloves garlic, roughly chopped

A good pinch of each: ground cloves, cardamom, caraway, mace, nutmeg, paprika

½ tsp ground ginger

½ tsp curcuma (turmeric), more if necessary

2 pinches of cinnamon

1 cup / 250 ml pineapple juice

Scant 1½ cups / 330 ml unsweetened coconut milk

4 cups / 1 liter vegetable broth (stock)

2 tbsp chopped fresh cilantro (coriander)

2 tbsp lemon juice

Method

Prep and cook time: 45 min

1. Wash the mussels thoroughly and remove the beards. Wash again; discard any opened mussels, as they are spoilt. Drain in a colander.

2. Heat the oil in a large pan and sauté the onions, garlic and chili until the onions and garlic are transparent. Add the spices and fry briefly, then take out of the pan, leaving 1 teaspoon of the spices in the pan. Add the pineapple juice, coconut milk and ⅔–1 cup (150–250 ml) of water and cook without a lid over a medium heat for about 10 minutes. Taste from time to time and add more water and spices if necessary to produce a creamy sauce.

3. Meanwhile, heat the broth (stock) in a large pan, add the mussels, cover and cook over a medium heat for 6–8 minutes, until the mussels have opened. Shake the pan vigorously from time to time. Discard any mussels that do not open.

4. Lift the mussels out of their cooking liquor. Stir the cilantro (coriander) into the curry sauce and add lemon juice to taste. Combine the mussels with the sauce and serve.

SHRIMP AND MANGO CURRY

Ingredients

2 mangoes

3 tbsp grated coconut

3 tbsp coconut milk

A good pinch of chili powder

2 tbsp curry powder

2 tbsp sesame oil, plus some for seasoning

1 carrot, finely diced

2 onions, finely diced

3 garlic cloves, very finely diced

2 stalks celery, with leaves, diced finely, reserve a few leaves

1 lb 2 oz / 500 g large shrimp or prawns

Juice of ½ lemon

Salt & freshly milled pepper

Method

Prep and cook time: 30 min

1. Peel the mangoes and cut the flesh away from the stone in slices about ¼ inch (5 mm) thick.

2. Put half the mango flesh into a blender with the grated coconut, coconut milk, chili powder, curry powder and 3 tablespoons of water and blend to a fine purée.

3. Heat the sesame oil and briefly sauté the diced vegetables. Add the shrimp and sauté briefly. Stir in the puréed mango sauce and simmer gently for about 8 minutes. If the sauce becomes too thick, thin with a little coconut milk or warm water.

4. Season the seafood curry with lemon juice, sesame oil, salt and pepper. Serve garnished with the remaining mango slices and celery leaves.

SALMON FILLET WITH COCONUT CURRY SAUCE

Ingredients

4 pieces salmon fillet, skin on

Juice of 1 lime

6 stems chard

Vegetable oil, for frying

1 tbsp butter

1 red chili pepper, deseeded and finely chopped

Salt and pepper

1 tbsp curry powder

½ cup / 125 ml coconut milk

Method

Prep and cook time: 25 min

1. Rub the lime juice into the salmon and set aside.

2. Strip the leaf from the stalk of the chards. Finely dice the stalk and shred the leaf.

3. Heat some oil and the butter in a skillet and gently cook the chard stalks and chili until soft. Turn up the heat, add the shredded leaves and cook for 2 minutes. Season with salt and pepper, remove from the skillet and set aside.

4. Add a little more oil to the pan and fry the salmon, skin side up, for 3 minutes then turn over and cook for 2 more minutes or until the fish is just cooked through. Remove the fish from the skillet and set aside in a warm place.

5. Fry the curry powder in the skillet for 1 minute then add the coconut milk. Let bubble, season with salt and pepper and cook for 2 minutes.

6. Serve the fish with the chard and onion on top and the sauce poured around.

CHINESE-STYLE COD

Ingredients

1½ cups / 250 g baby corn

8 scallions (spring onions), cut diagonally into 2 inch / 4-cm lengths

1 red bell pepper, cut into strips

2 carrots, thinly sliced on the diagonal

2 stalks celery, sliced

2 tbsp vegetable oil

2 garlic cloves, thinly sliced

8 cod fillets (about 1 lb 12 oz / 800 g total)

2 tbsp rice wine

2 tbsp soy sauce

2 tbsp fish sauce

Salt and pepper

Method
Prep and cook time: 45 min

1. Bring a large pot of salted water to a boil and blanch the baby corn, scallions (spring onions), bell pepper, carrots and celery for around 4 minutes until al dente.

2. Meanwhile, heat the oil in a skillet or wok, briefly fry the garlic just until fragrant, 30 seconds; remove the garlic with a slotted spoon to a plate, and return the skillet to the heat.

3. Add the fish fillets to the skillet and fry until golden brown on one side. Turn the fish over and add 4 tbsp of water, the rice wine, soy sauce and fish sauce.

4. Return the garlic to the skillet, reduce the heat and simmer for a further 1–2 minutes until the fish is cooked. Season with salt and pepper.

5. Drain the vegetables and arrange on plates. Top with the fish fillets and sauce.

TANDOORI FISH MASALA

Ingredients

4 fish fillets, e.g. sea bream, cod, each weighing 7 oz / 200 g

Salt

2 tbsp lemon juice

2 tbsp ghee or clarified butter, melted

For the marinade:

2 cups / 400 g yogurt

3 tbsp vinegar

1 large onion, finely chopped

3–5 garlic cloves, crushed

½ tsp freshly grated ginger

½–1 tsp curcuma (turmeric)

1 pinch of each: salt, ground coriander, garam masala, chili powder

Pepper, according to taste

½ red chili, deseeded and cut into rings

Garnish: 1 tbsp scallion (spring onion) rings and 1 tbsp lime zest

Method

Prep and cook time: 40 min plus 2 hours to marinate

1. Rub the fish fillets with salt and drizzle lemon juice over the top. Place the fish in a baking dish, greased with ghee or clarified butter.

2. For the marinade, mix all the ingredients together with 1–2 tablespoons water. Pour over the fish and place in the refrigerator for 2 hours. Turn the fish from time to time.

3. Pre-heat the oven to 350°F (180°C / Gas Mark 4). Put the fish in the oven and cook for about 15–20 minutes. Add a little water if needed. Before serving, place the fish under a pre-heated broiler (grill) for a few minutes to brown (according to taste).

4. Divide between 4 bowls, placing a fish fillet in the center of each bowl. Scatter a few chili and scallion (spring onion) rings over the fish and sprinkle some lime zest on the top. Serve hot.

TIGER SHRIMPS MAHARAJA STYLE

Ingredients

3 tbsp clarified butter or oil

2 garlic cloves, finely chopped

Thumb-size piece ginger, peeled and finely chopped

1 red chili pepper, deseeded and finely chopped

1 tsp garam masala

2 cups / 500 ml coconut milk

1 cup / 250 ml fish broth (stock) or water

20 tiger shrimps, peeled with tails left on

Juice of 1 lime

1 tbsp chopped cilantro (fresh coriander)

Salt and pepper

Parsley sprigs, to garnish

Method

Prep and cook time: 20 min

1. Heat the butter in a wide pan and gently cook the garlic, ginger and chili pepper until soft but not brown.

2. Add the garam masala, cook for 1 minute then pour in the coconut milk and fish broth (stock) and simmer gently for about 10 minutes.

3. Add the shrimps and simmer for 5 more minutes or until the shrimps are cooked through. Stir in the lime juice, season with salt and pepper and add the chopped cilantro (coriander).

CLAM AND MANGOSTEEN CURRY

Ingredients

2 lbs 4 oz / 1kg fresh clams, or mixed shellfish

6 tbsp oil

3–4 cloves garlic, finely chopped

2 chilies, deseeded and chopped in half

1 cup / 240 ml water

½ cup / 120 ml fish broth (stock)

5 tbsp finely chopped Thai basil

Salt & freshly ground pepper

1–2 mangosteens

1–2 tbsp lime juice

¼ bunch chives, for garnish

6–8 kaffir lime leaves, for garnish

Method

Prep and cook time: 40 min

1. Soak the clams in a bowl of cold water for 20 minutes, to remove any sand. Scrub the clams and throw away any that have opened slightly at this stage.

2. Heat 4 tablespoons oil and sweat the garlic and one of the chilies without browning. Add the clams and heat for three minutes, until all the shells have opened. Throw away any that do not open at this stage.

3. Add the water and fish broth (stock) and cook over a low heat for 4 minutes. Remove the clams to a bowl and strain the liquid through a fine sieve to remove any last traces of sand, then return the liquid and the clams to the pan. Add the basil and the rest of the olive oil and season well with pepper and a little salt.

4. Chop the mangosteen flesh into pieces and purée finely. Put into a pan, add a little of the clam cooking liquid and heat. Add the lime juice to taste.

5. Spoon the mangosteen puree into bowls, add the clams and serve garnished with slices of the remaining chili, chives and lime leaves.

SPICY KING PRAWNS

Ingredients

1 tbsp vegetable oil

1 inch / 3 cm piece fresh ginger, peeled and grated

2 garlic cloves, minced

2 scallions (spring onions) and chopped

1 lb / 450 g raw large shrimp (prawns), peeled and deveined

1 tbsp tomato paste (purée)

2 tsp chili bean sauce

1 tsp cider vinegar

1 tsp sugar

2 tsp sesame oil

Cilantro (fresh coriander) leaves, to garnish

Method
Prep and cook time: 20 min

1. Heat the oil in a large skillet or wok. Add the ginger, garlic and scallions (spring onions) and stir-fry for 20 seconds.

2. Add the shrimp (prawns) and stir-fry for 1 minute.

3. Add the tomato paste (purée), chili bean sauce, cider vinegar, sugar and sesame oil and stir-fry for another few minutes. Serve at once, garnished with cilantro (coriander).

MONKFISH AND GREEN COCONUT CURRY SAUCE

Ingredients

For the curry paste:

1 shallot, peeled

1 clove garlic, peeled

1 green chili

1 tbsp cilantro (coriander) leaves

1 tsp cilantro root, chopped

1 pinch galangal, ground

4 peppercorns

½ tsp coriander seeds

2 lb 4oz / 1 kg monk fish fillets

Salt

4 tbsp lemon juice

2 tbsp light soy sauce

Scant 1 cup / 200 ml unsweetened coconut milk

3–4 tbsp oil

4–5 scallions (spring onions), white part only, cut into rings

1 zucchini (courgette), thinly sliced

4 kaffir lime leaves, finely chopped

3 sprigs Thai basil

Method

Prep and cook time: 30 min plus 30 mins to marinate

1. For the curry paste, place all ingredients in a mortar and grind to a smooth paste.

2. Skin the fish and cut into 1 inch (2.5 cm) pieces. Marinate the fish pieces with the salt, lemon juice and soy sauce for about 30 minutes.

3. Heat the coconut milk over a low heat and simmer for 5 minutes. Heat the oil in a wok and fry the fish for about 4 minutes. Pour in the coconut milk and the curry paste and the rest of the marinade. (If you don't use all the curry paste, you can put the remainder in a jar and keep it in the refrigerator for a few days.) Reduce the heat and simmer the fish for 3 minutes.

4. Add the scallions (spring onions), zucchini (courgette), some basil leaves and the lime leaves and cook for a further 3 minutes.

5. Scoop the curry onto warmed plates and garnish with the remaining basil leaves. Serve with basmati rice.

FRIED FISH WITH GINGER, CARROTS AND SNOW PEAS

Ingredients

1 lb / 450 g firm white fish fillet such as cod or halibut, cut into strips

Salt and pepper

2 tbsp cornstarch (cornflour)

$^2/_3$ cup / 150 ml vegetable oil

1 inch / 3 cm piece fresh ginger root, peeled and grated

2 tbsp sesame oil

3 carrots, thinly sliced on the diagonal

7 oz / 200 g snow peas (mangetout)

4 scallions (spring onions), thinly sliced

2 tbsp rice wine or dry sherry

2 tsp sugar

2 tbsp black bean sauce

2 tbsp sweet chilli sauce

Method

Prep and cook time: 25 min

1. Season the fish with salt and ground black pepper and sprinkle over the cornstarch (cornflour) to coat.

2. Heat the oil in a wok or skillet until very hot then add the fish and fry for a few minutes until almost cooked through.

3. Remove the fish from the oil with a slotted spoon and drain on paper towels.

4. Return the wok the heat and fry the ginger for 1 minute then add the sesame oil, heat until smoking and add the carrots.

5. Stir fry for 2 minutes then add the snow peas (mangetout) and scallions (spring onions) and cook for 1 more minute.

6. Pour in the rice wine or sherry, sugar, and 2 tbsp water. Heat through then return the fish to the skillet and cook gently for 1 minute, taking care not to break up the pieces of fish.

7. Quickly stir through the black bean sauce and chilli sauce and serve immediately.

SHRIMP IN BATTER WITH CASHEWS AND RICE

Ingredients

½ cup / 75 g cashews

1 cup / 100 g all-purpose (plain) flour

2 eggs, separated

½ cup / 125 ml dry white wine

Vegetable oil for deep frying

1 lb 6 oz / 600 g large shrimp (prawns), peeled and deveined

Salt & freshly ground pepper

Method

Prep and cook time: 30 min plus 30 min resting time

1. Toast the cashew nuts in a dry skillet until golden brown.

2. In a medium bowl, whisk together the flour, egg yolks and wine to make a smooth batter and season with salt and pepper. Let rest for 30 minutes.

3. In another medium bowl, beat the egg whites until stiff and fold into the rested batter.

4. Heat the oil in a deep fat fryer to 180°C / 350°F. The oil is hot enough when bubbles rise from the handle of a wooden spoon dipped into the fat.

5. Working in batches, dip the shrimp (prawns) in the batter, shake off the excess and deep-fry for about 3 minutes until golden brown. Drain on paper towels and keep warm.

6. Serve the shrimp with the cashews and boiled rice.

SALMON CURRY WITH MANGO

Ingredients

3 tbsp clarified butter or oil

1 onion, very finely chopped

2 garlic cloves, finely chopped

½ tsp curcuma (turmeric)

Thumb-size piece ginger, peeled and finely chopped

1 green chili pepper, deseeded and finely chopped

3 cups / 750 ml fish broth (stock)

Juice of 2 limes

1 lb 8 oz / 650 g salmon fillet, skinned and cut into chunks

2 mangoes, peeled, stones removed and cut into chunks

1 cup / 100 g desiccated coconut

2 tbsp chopped cilantro (fresh coriander) plus some to garnish

2 tbsp black mustard seeds, lightly toasted

Method

Prep and cook time: 30 min

1. Heat the butter in a wide pan and gently fry the onion until soft but not brown.

2. Add the garlic, curcuma (turmeric), ginger and chili pepper and cook for 2 more minutes then add the fish broth (stock) and lime juice.

3. Bring to a boil then turn the heat down and add the salmon, mango and coconut. Simmer for 10 minutes or until the salmon is cooked through, then stir in the chopped cilantro (coriander).

4. Serve with the mustard seeds scattered over and garnish with cilantro sprigs.

VEGETARIAN AND VEGETABLE DISHES

CAULIFLOWER CURRY WITH CHICKPEAS

Ingredients

3 tbsp oil

1 onion, finely chopped

2 garlic cloves, chopped

Thumb-size piece of ginger, peeled and grated

1 tsp chili powder

3 tsp garam masala

1 lb / 450 g potatoes, diced

1 lb / 450 g cauliflower florets

1 cup / 250 ml vegetable broth (stock) or water

1 cup / 250 ml yogurt

1½ cups / 300 g canned chickpeas, drained

2 handfuls spinach, washed and roughly chopped

3 tbsp lemon juice

1 tsp paprika

Salt and pepper

Lemon wedges, to garnish

Method

Prep and cook time: 45 min

1. Heat the oil in a large skillet and gently fry the onion until soft but not brown.

2. Add the garlic, ginger, chili powder and garam masala and fry for 2 minutes.

3. Stir in the potatoes and cook gently for 5 minutes. Add the cauliflower, cook for 2 minutes then add the vegetable broth (stock) and yogurt and simmer over a low heat for 15 minutes.

4. Add the chickpeas and spinach and cook for a further 5 minutes then stir in the lemon juice and season with salt and pepper. Serve garnished with lemon wedges.

CURRY MEE WITH TOFU

Ingredients

14 oz / 400 g tofu, smoked or plain according to taste

9 oz / 250 g Chinese egg noodles

5 tbsp vegetable oil

Scant 1 cup / 200 ml unsweetened coconut milk, more if necessary

2 red chilies, deseeded and very finely chopped

2 cloves garlic, finely chopped

½ tsp pepper

2 tbsp curry powder

1 handful bean sprouts

2 tbsp light soy sauce

1 tbsp vinegar

1 tbsp sugar

2 tbsp fish sauce

Method

Prep and cook time: 35 min

1. Dice the tofu and drain on paper towel.

2. Put the noodles into a bowl and soak in lukewarm water.

3. Heat the oil and brown the tofu on all sides for 2–3 minutes. Add the coconut milk.

4. Add the chilies and the garlic to the pan with the spices and bring to a boil.

5. Drain the noodles, break into smaller pieces if necessary and add to the pan. Cook gently in the hot sauce for 3–4 minutes, until done. Mix in the bean sprouts and warm in the sauce. Add soy sauce, vinegar, sugar and fish sauce to taste. Divide between 4 small bowls and serve hot.

WHITE CABBAGE CURRY

Ingredients

3 tbsp clarified butter or oil

Thumb-size piece ginger, peeled and grated

2 tsp garam masala

1 tsp ground coriander

1 tsp curcuma (turmeric)

1 tsp ground cumin

2 bay leaves

1 small white cabbage, trimmed and shredded

1 lb / 450 g waxy potatoes, peeled and cubed

Salt and pepper

1 cup / 150 g frozen peas

2 large tomatoes, deseeded and diced

Method

Prep and cook time: 25 min

1. Heat the clarified butter or oil in a large skillet and gently fry the ginger, garam masala, coriander, curcuma (turmeric), cumin and bay leaves for 3 minutes, stirring all the time.

2. Stir in the cabbage and the potatoes, cook for 2 minutes then add about ½ cup (125 ml) of water. Season with salt and pepper and cook for 10 minutes, stirring from time to time. Add more water if needed.

3. Add the peas and tomatoes, cook for 5 more minutes then serve accompanied with rice.

ORIENTAL NOODLE BAKE

Ingredients

8 oz / 225 g mie noodles

1 clove garlic, chopped

1²/₃ cups / 400 ml coconut milk

2 tbsp soy sauce

Cayenne pepper

3 eggs

¼ oz / 5 g dried mu err mushrooms, soaked in water according to package instructions

3 tbsp butter

8 oz / 225 g snow peas (mangetout), halved

2 carrots, pared into very thin slices with a peeler

4 scallions (spring onions), chopped into rings

1 red bell pepper, deseeded and finely sliced

2 tbsp chopped cilantro (fresh coriander)

2–3 tbsp bread crumbs

Cilantro (fresh coriander) leaves, to garnish

Method

Prep and cook time: 1 hour

1. Preheat the oven to 200C (400F / Gas Mark 6).

2. Cook the noodles according to the package instructions, refresh and drain.

3. Mix together the garlic and coconut milk, season to taste with some of the soy sauce and some cayenne pepper and stir in the eggs.

4. Drain the mushrooms, pat dry and chop into fine slices.

5. Heat 1 tbsp of butter in a skillet and fry the snow peas (mangetout) with 2–3 tbsp of water for 2–3 minutes. Add the carrots and fry for a further 2 minutes.

6. Stir in the scallions (spring onions), bell peppers, mushrooms and chopped cilantro (fresh coriander) and season with soy sauce.

7. Place the noodles into a greased ovenproof dish and spread the vegetable mixture on top.

8. Pour over the coconut sauce, sprinkle with bread crumbs, dot with the remaining butter and bake for about 20 minutes.

9. Garnish with cilantro (fresh coriander) leaves and serve.

LENTIL STEW

Ingredients

1 cup / 150 g cashew nuts

4 tbsp vegetable oil

½ cup / 100 g split red lentils, washed
and drained

½ tsp ground coriander

½ tsp ground cloves

½ tsp cumin

1 leek, sliced

1 carrot, cut into batons

1 potato, peeled and cut into chunks

2 cups / 500 ml vegetable broth (stock)

1 cup / 200 g canned chickpeas,
drained and rinsed

Salt and pepper

Cilantro leaves (fresh coriander),
to garnish

Method
Prep and cook time: 40 min

1. Roast the cashew nuts in a dry skillet
until lightly browned then set aside.

2. Heat the oil in a large pan and stir in
the lentils, coriander, cloves and cumin.
Cook for 2 minutes then add the leek,
carrot and potato.

3. Pour in the broth (stock) and chickpeas,
season with salt and pepper and simmer
gently for 20 minutes, stirring from time
to time, or until the lentils are tender.

4. Add the cashew nuts, heat through and
serve garnished with cilantro (coriander)
leaves.

LENTIL CURRY WITH PANEER

Ingredients

2 tbsp ghee or clarified butter

2 onions, finely chopped

2 cloves garlic, finely chopped

1 tsp curcuma (turmeric)

Pinch of ground cloves

Pinch of ground cumin

Pinch of ground allspice

2 curry leaves

1 cup / 250 ml unsweetened coconut milk

1¾ cups / about 400 ml vegetable broth (stock)

1 cup / 200 g black lentils

1 cup / 200 g red lentils

Salt & freshly milled pepper

7 oz / 200 g paneer cheese

Method

Prep and cook time: 40 min

1. Heat the ghee (or clarified butter) and sauté the onions and garlic, add the spices and sauté briefly before pouring in the coconut milk. Stir in a little broth (stock) and the black lentils, cover and simmer gently for about 10 minutes.

2. Add the red lentils and a little more broth. Simmer for a further 15 minutes or so, stirring occasionally, until the lentils are tender and add the rest of the broth as necessary.

3. Remove the curry leaves and season to taste with salt and pepper.

4. Dice the paneer and add to the curry. Serve with flatbread.

EGGPLANT AND SNOW PEA CURRY

Ingredients

1 cup / 150 g snow peas (mangetout), trimmed

1½ inch / 4 cm lemongrass

1 green chili

1 clove garlic, peeled

1 kaffir lime leaf

2 shallots, finely chopped

2 tbsp oil

1 cup / 250 ml vegetable broth (stock)

1 cup / 250 ml unsweetened coconut milk

6 Thai eggplants (aubergines), roughly chopped

1 lb 2 oz / 500 g sweet potatoes, peeled and diced

½ an untreated lime, juice and zest

Light soy sauce

Honey

Salt

Method

Prep and cook time: 30 min

1. Blanch the snow peas (mangetout) in boiling salted water until al dente. Place immediately into cold water then drain.

2. Crush the lemongrass, chili, garlic and kaffir lime leaf to a smooth paste using a pestle and mortar.

3 Sauté the shallots in hot oil with the curry paste. Pour in the vegetable broth (stock) and the coconut milk and simmer for about 5 minutes. Add the eggplant and the sweet potatoes and simmer for 10 minutes, stirring occasionally. Add the lime juice, lime zest and snow peas and season to taste with soy sauce, honey and salt before serving.

LENTIL AND POTATO CURRY

Ingredients

2 tsp ghee or clarified butter

1 onion, finely chopped

2 clove garlic, finely chopped

Walnut-size piece fresh ginger, peeled and grated

1 tsp curcuma (turmeric)

½ tsp cayenne pepper

½ tsp ground coriander

½ tsp cumin

1 lb / 450 g waxy potatoes, roughly chopped

8 oz / 225 g pumpkin flesh, roughly chopped

1¼ cups / 250 g lentils, rinsed and drained

1¼ cups / 250 g canned tomatoes, chopped

Salt

2 tbsp cilantro (fresh coriander), to garnish

Method

Prep and cook time: 50 min

1. Sweat the onion and garlic with the ginger, curcuma (turmeric), cayenne pepper, coriander and cumin in hot ghee for 4–5 minutes, stirring occasionally.

2. Add the potatoes, pumpkin, lentils, tomatoes and just enough water to cover all the ingredients. Cover and simmer gently for 30–40 minutes, stirring occasionally and ensuring that the pan does not boil dry.

3. Season with salt and serve garnished with cilantro (fresh coriander) leaves.

VEGETABLE KORMA

Ingredients

1 onion, finely chopped

2 tbsp ghee or clarified butter

1 tsp curcuma (turmeric)

½ tsp cumin

½ tsp ground ginger

$^2/_3$ cup / 150 ml vegetable broth (stock)

2 cups / 600 g cauliflower florets

$^2/_3$ cup / 100 g peeled almonds,
roughly chopped

2 carrots, peeled and roughly chopped

2 cups / 200 g canned chickpeas,
rinsed and drained

$^2/_3$ cup / 150 ml yogurt

8 oz / 225 g fresh spinach, rinsed
and spun dry

Salt and freshly ground pepper

Method

Prep and cook time: 35 min

1. Sweat the onion in hot ghee or clarified butter. Add the curcuma (turmeric), cumin and ginger and continue frying for a few minutes then pour in the vegetable broth (stock).

2. Add the cauliflower, almonds, carrots and chickpeas, season with salt, cover and simmer for about 15 minutes, stirring occasionally, until the vegetables are cooked through.

3. Stir in the yogurt and spinach, remove from the heat and season with salt and pepper.

4. Divide the Korma between 4 plates and serve with rice.

EGGPLANTS IN PEANUT SAUCE

Ingredients

6 tbsp oil

2 lb / 900 g baby eggplants (aubergines)

2 onions, chopped

2 garlic cloves, chopped

Thumb-size piece ginger, peeled and chopped

2 red chili peppers, deseeded and chopped

2 tsp coriander seeds

1 tsp cumin seeds

1 tsp mustard seeds

2 tbsp desiccated coconut

1 tbsp tamarind paste

3 tbsp tomato paste (purée)

Salt and pepper

12 green beans, halved

1¾ cups / 200 g peanuts, chopped

Method

Prep and cook time: 40 min

1. Heat the oil in a wide pan and gently cook the whole eggplants (aubergines) until tender. Do not allow them to brown.

2. Remove the eggplants from the pan and set half aside. Scoop the flesh from the other half and set aside.

3. Cook the onions very gently until soft but not brown then add the garlic, ginger, chili, coriander seeds, cumin seeds and mustard seeds and cook for 2 minutes.

4. Stir in the coconut, tamarind paste and tomato paste (purée) and cook for 2 minutes.

5. Add the chopped eggplant flesh and half a cup of water, season with salt and pepper and simmer very gently, stirring from time to time for 20 minutes. Add a little more water during cooking if needed.

6. Meanwhile, blanch the beans in boiling salted water for 3 minutes and add to the pan.

7. Lightly toast the peanuts in a dry pan and add to the curry. Return the whole eggplants to the pan, heat though and serve.

RICE NOODLES WITH CABBAGE AND RED COCONUT SAUCE

Ingredients

1 tbsp sesame oil

1 shallot, finely chopped

2 garlic cloves, finely chopped

½ tsp chili powder

½ tsp curcuma (turmeric)

½ tsp ground paprika

½ tsp ground five-spice powder

Scant 1 cup / 200 ml coconut milk

2 tbsp lime juice

½ cup / 125 ml vegetable broth (stock)

1 lb / 450 g Savoy cabbage, chopped into strips or torn into bite-size pieces

½ cup / 50 g soybean shoots

8 oz / 225 g rice noodles

Salt

Method

Prep and cook time: 30 min

1. Fry the shallots and garlic in sesame oil.

2. Add the chili powder, curcuma (turmeric), paprika and five-spice powder and fry briefly then add the coconut milk, lime juice and vegetable broth (stock). Simmer gently for about 5 minutes and season with salt.

3. Add the Savoy cabbage and simmer gently for a further 5–7 minutes. Last of all, add the soybean shoots and warm through for 1–2 minutes.

4. Cook the rice noodles in plenty of water according to the package instructions and drain.

5. Divide the noodles between four bowls and top with the Savoy cabbage in coconut sauce.

DHAL

Ingredients

1 cup / 300 g red lentils, rinsed

2 bay leaves

1 tsp salt

1 cinnamon stick

3 tbsp clarified butter or oil

1 onion, finely chopped

2 garlic cloves, finely chopped

Thumb-size piece ginger, peeled and grated

2 tsp curcuma (turmeric)

1 tsp ground cumin

½ tsp garam masala

1 tsp chili powder

Juice of 1 lemon

1 tsp salt

1 tbsp chopped cilantro (fresh coriander), plus some to garnish

Poppadums, to serve

Method

Prep and cook time: 30 min

1. Put the lentils, bay leaves, salt and cinnamon stick in pan with 3 cups of water, bring to a boil and simmer for 15 minutes, stirring from time to time, or until the lentils are soft. Add more water if needed to prevent the mixture becoming dry. Discard the bay leaves and cinnamon stick and set aside.

2. Heat the butter in a pan and gently fry the onion until soft but not brown then add the garlic, ginger, curcuma (turmeric), cumin, garam masala and chili powder. Cook for 2 minutes then stir in the cooked lentils.

3. Add the lemon juice, season with salt and pepper and gently cook for 5 more minutes, stirring all the time to prevent burning.

4. Stir in the chopped cilantro (coriander) and serve garnished with the cilantro leaves and the poppadums alongside.

PUNJABI STYLE CHICKPEAS

Ingredients

10 oz / 300 g dried chickpeas, soaked overnight and drained

4 tbsp olive oil

4 shallots, sliced into rings

1 garlic clove, sliced

½ tsp cumin

½ tsp ground coriander

1 tsp garam masala

½ tsp curcuma (turmeric)

8 oz / 225 g floury potatoes, peeled and chopped

2 tomatoes, roughly chopped

2 chili peppers

2 tbsp cilantro (fresh coriander), chopped

Cayenne pepper

Salt

Method

Prep and cook time: 2 hours 20 min plus overnight soaking

1. Cover the chickpeas with 5 cups (1¼ liters) of water and simmer over a low heat for 1½ hours until soft.

2. Fry the shallots in hot oil until golden brown. Remove 1 tbsp from the pan and reserve to garnish.

3. Add the garlic, cumin, ground coriander, garam masala and curcuma (turmeric) to the shallots in the pan and fry briefly.

4. Add the potatoes, drained chickpeas and a scant ½ cup (about 100 ml) of water.

5. Add the tomatoes and chili peppers, cover and simmer gently for about 30 minutes, stirring occasionally. Add a little more water if necessary.

6. Season to taste with salt and cayenne pepper and stir in the chopped cilantro (fresh coriander).

7. Spoon into bowls and serve garnished with the reserved shallots.

STIR-FRIED VEGETABLES WITH TOFU

Ingredients

2 tsp vegetable oil, divided

1 lb / 450 g extra firm tofu, cut into cubes

4 shallots, quartered

2 garlic cloves, crushed

1 inch / 3-cm piece fresh ginger root, peeled and grated

1 cup / 200 g baby corn

8 oz / 200 g snow peas (mangetout)

2 cups / 200 g bean sprouts

8 oz / 200 g oyster and/or shiitake mushrooms, halved if large

1 cup / 225 ml vegetable broth (stock)

1 tbsp dark brown sugar

1 tbsp light soy sauce

2 tsp cornstarch (cornflour), mixed to a smooth paste in 2 tbsp water

Method

Prep and cook time: 20 min

1. In a nonstick skillet, heat 1 teaspoon of the oil over medium-high heat until hot. Add the tofu and cook, gently for about 4 minutes, tossing until lightly golden. Transfer to a plate and set aside.

2. Meanwhile, heat the remaining teaspoon of oil in a large skillet or wok. Add the shallots, garlic, ginger, corn, snow peas, bean sprouts and mushrooms. Cook for 5 minutes, stirring frequently.

3. Add the tofu to the wok. Pour in the broth (stock), sugar, soy sauce and cornstarch (cornflour) mixture. Heat to boiling and cook for 2 minutes until the sauce thickens. Serve at once.

VEGETABLE NOODLES

Ingredients

For the curry paste:

1 red chili

1 clove garlic

¾ inch / 2 cm galangal, peeled

Good pinch grated zest of kaffir lime

1 tsp shrimp paste

For the vegetable noodles:

12–14 oz / 350–400 g mie noodles

8–10 oz / 250–300 g shiitake
mushrooms, sliced

2 red bell peppers, cut into strips

1 scallion (spring onion)
cut into strips

1 tbsp vegetable oil

¾–1 cup / 200 ml coconut milk

3 sprigs Thai basil

1 tsp fish sauce

Salt & freshly milled pepper

Method
Prep and cook time: 25 min

1. Put all the curry paste ingredients into a mortar and grind to a paste.

2. Cook the noodles in plenty of boiling, salted water according to the package instructions until al dente.

3. Heat the vegetable oil and sauté the vegetables. Stir in 1–2 tablespoons of curry paste and the coconut milk and simmer for 3–5 minutes.

4. Strip the Thai basil leaves from the stalks and add to the vegetables.

5. Season to taste with salt, pepper and fish sauce and add a little water if necessary.

6. Drain the noodles and put into bowls. Divide the vegetables between the bowls and serve hot.

POTATO CURRY WITH ZUCCHINI AND CASHEW NUTS

Ingredients

2 lb 4 oz / 1 kg boiling potatoes, peeled and diced

2 tbsp ghee or clarified butter

1 lb / 450 g small zucchini (courgettes), cut into cubes

1 red onion, chopped

1 clove garlic, chopped

1 oz / 25 g ginger, peeled and chopped

1 tbsp curry powder, according to taste

1 tsp ground cumin

Salt & freshly milled pepper

10 oz / 300 g tomatoes, deseeded and quartered

2 cups / 500 ml vegetable broth (stock)

1 tbsp potato starch

½ cup / 60 g cashew nuts, roasted

Method

Prep and cook time: 45 min

1. Blanch the potatoes in boiling salted water for 8 minutes, then drain.

2. Fry the potatoes in hot ghee or clarified butter. Add the zucchini and sauté, then stir in the garlic, onion and ginger and fry. Season with curry powder, cumin, salt and pepper. Now add the tomatoes and pour in the vegetable broth (stock). Simmer for 15–20 minutes.

3. Mix the potato starch to a paste with a drop of cold water, then stir the mixture into the hot curry. Bring to a boil, then simmer and season to taste.

4. Sprinkle a few roasted cashew nuts over the top and serve on warmed plates.

NOODLES WITH PEANUT SAUCE AND TOFU

Ingredients

For the peanut sauce:

½ cup / 100 g unsalted peanuts, toasted and finely chopped

2 shallots, finely chopped

2 garlic cloves, finely chopped

3 tbsp sweet soy sauce

Juice of ½ lemon

1 tsp chili paste

1 tbsp sugar

2 tbsp groundnut oil

1¼ cups / 300 ml coconut milk

Salt

For the noodles:

1 lb / 450 g oriental wheat flour noodles

8 oz / 225 g red cabbage, chopped into fine strips

1 red bell pepper, deseeded and chopped into strips.

4 scallions (spring onions), chopped into rings

4 carrots, chopped into fine strips

8 oz / 225 g tofu, chopped into cubes

Method
Prep and cook time: 40 min

1. To make the sauce, place the peanuts, shallots, garlic, soy sauce, lemon juice, chili paste and sugar in a tall mixing beaker and purée to a creamy paste using a hand-held blender.

2. Heat the groundnut oil in a pan and briefly fry the peanut paste. Pour in the coconut milk, stir until smooth then simmer for about 3 minutes until slightly thickened. Season with salt.

3. Cook the noodles according to the package instructions. Drain and divide between four plates.

4. Spoon the sauce over the noodles, scatter with the red cabbage and pepper strips, scallions (spring onions), carrot strips and tofu, and serve.

FRIED RICE WITH ONIONS, EGG AND MUSHROOMS

Ingredients

1 1/3 cups / 250 g long-grain rice

3 tbsp vegetable oil

8 scallions (spring onions), sliced diagonally into rings (reserve a few for garnish)

2 cups / 250 g halved mushrooms

6 eggs

Freshly ground pepper, to taste

2 tbsp light soy sauce, plus more to taste

Sliced scallion (spring onion), to garnish

Method

Prep and cook time: 40 min

1. Cook the rice according to the instructions on the package and let cool completely.

2. Heat the oil in a wok or skillet. Add the scallion (spring onion) rings and stir-fry for 2 minutes. Add the mushrooms and stir-fry until all liquid has evaporated.

3. Add the rice and cook, stirring, about 3 minutes, then push the rice mixture to the edges of the wok.

4. In a small bowl, whisk the eggs and season with pepper and 2 tbsp soy sauce. Pour into the center of the wok and cook quickly, stirring constantly. Lightly mix the eggs through the rice and season with soy sauce, to taste. Scatter with the reserved scallion rings and serve at once.

RIBBON NOODLES WITH COCONUT CURRY SAUCE

Ingredients

For the curry paste:

2 dried chilies

1 shallot, peeled

¾ inch / 2 cm coriander root

¾ inch / 2 cm lemongrass

Good pinch of cumin seeds

½ tsp curcuma (turmeric)

1 lb 2 oz / 500 g ribbon noodles

1 tbsp oil

1 onion, finely chopped

1–2 cloves garlic, finely chopped

Juice and finely grated zest of 1 lime

1¾ cup / 400 ml unsweetened coconut milk

1–2 tbsp fish sauce

Salt & pepper

Sugar

Parsley leaves, to garnish

Method

Prep and cook time: 30 min

1. Put all the ingredients for the curry paste into a mortar and crush to a paste.

2. Cook the ribbon noodles according to the package instructions until al dente.

3. Meanwhile, heat the oil and sauté the chopped onion and garlic until translucent. Add the lime zest and stir in the coconut milk. Stir in the lime juice, curry paste and fish sauce and season to taste with salt, pepper and sugar. Simmer the sauce gently for about 5 minutes, until it has a creamy consistency. Remove from the heat and blend with a hand blender.

4. Drain the cooked noodles, mix at once with the coconut curry sauce and serve garnished with parsley leaves.

DHAL WITH COCONUT AND RAISINS

Ingredients

1–2 tbsp raisins

9 oz / 250 g split chickpeas
(channa dal)

1–2 tsp curcuma (turmeric)

A good pinch of chili powder

2 green chilies

2 tbsp jaggery (or brown sugar)

½ tsp ground coriander

½ tsp ground cumin

1–2 tsp garam masala

A good pinch of salt

2–3 tbsp ghee or clarified butter

1 cup / 100 g coconut flakes

Method

Prep and cook time: 1 hour

1. Wash the raisins and put into a cup of hot water to soak. Wash the chickpeas in cold water and put into a pan with the curcuma (turmeric), chili powder and 4 cups (1 liter) of water. Bring to a boil, cover and cook over a low heat for about 30 minutes.

2. Trim and halve the chilies, remove the inner ribs and the seeds if you wish, and cut into rings. Stir into the chickpeas with the jaggery, coriander, cumin and 1 tsp garam masala. Add the salt and cook for a further 10–15 minutes, until the chickpeas are very soft.

3. Heat the ghee (or clarified butter) in a skillet and lightly toast the rest of the garam masala and the coconut flakes. Mix into the dhal with the drained raisins. Spoon into bowls and serve with rice.

QUICK VEGETABLE CURRY

Ingredients

2 cups / 300 g green beans, trimmed

4 carrots, peeled and cut into batons

3 cups / 600 g broccoli, cut into florets

Oil

1–2 tbsp yellow curry paste, from a jar

2 garlic cloves, finely chopped

1 can coconut milk

1 red bell pepper, de-seeded and cut into strips

Chili powder, according to taste

Salt

Cilantro (coriander) sprigs, to garnish

Method

Prep and cook time: 35 min

1. Blanch the beans for 8 minutes in boiling, salted water, the carrots for 5 minutes and the broccoli florets for 4 minutes. Drain the vegetables well.

2. Heat the curry paste with 1 tablespoon of oil in a skillet. Sauté the garlic, then pour in the coconut milk. Bring to a boil, then reduce the heat and add the bell pepper. Simmer for about 3 minutes.

3. Add the broccoli, green beans and carrots and simmer for a further 2–3 minutes. Season to taste with chili powder and salt.

4. Garnish the vegetable curry with fresh cilantro (coriander) sprigs and serve with rice.

CHEESE AND BROCCOLI TIKKIS

Ingredients

1 tbsp oil plus oil for frying

¾ cup / 125 g finely chopped onions

2 cloves garlic, finely chopped

1–2 green chilies, finely chopped

1½ cups / 300 g broccoli florets, finely chopped

Salt

2–3 tbsp cornstarch (cornflour)

¾ cup / 70 g finely grated cheese

9 oz / 250 g baking potatoes, cooked and mashed

2 cups / 100 g breadcrumbs

For the yogurt dip:

Generous 1 cup / 300 g plain yogurt

1 tsp tandoori masala spices mix

Method

Prep and cook time: 1 hour

1. Heat 1 tablespoon of oil in a skillet and sauté the onions, garlic and chili. Add the broccoli and cook for 4–5 minutes, then season with salt. Stir in the cornstarch (cornflour) and the cheese, mix well, then let cool.

2. Combine with the mashed potatoes. Divide into 8 equal portions and form into round patties.

3. Coat the patties with breadcrumbs. Heat the frying oil in a large skillet and fry the tikkis on both sides until golden brown.

4. To make the yogurt dip, simply mix the yogurt with a teaspoonful of tandoori masala spices mix and serve with the tikkis.

INDIAN RICE SALAD

Ingredients

1 cup / 200 g long grain rice

½ cup / 125 ml vegetable oil

4 onions, very finely sliced

2 garlic cloves, chopped

1 tsp salt

1 tsp sugar

2 tsp black onion seeds

8 cardamom pods

8 curry leaves

Salt and pepper

Method

Prep and cook time: 30 min

1. Cook the rice according to packet instructions.

2. While the rice is cooking, heat the oil in a skillet and gently fry the onions and garlic with the salt and sugar, stirring from time to time, until they have started to caramelize and brown – this will take about 15 minutes.

3. Stir in the onion seeds, cardamom pods and curry leaves and cook for 3 more minutes.

4. When the rice is cooked, drain well and rinse then add to the onion mixture. Stir well and season with salt and pepper.

BOMBAY ALOO

Ingredients

6 large potatoes, peeled and cut into chunks

4 tbsp clarified butter or oil

1 onion, finely chopped

1 tsp cumin seeds

2 tsp black onion seeds

1 tsp mustard seeds

1 tsp fenugreek seeds

½ tsp curcuma (turmeric)

1 tsp garam masala

2 red chili peppers, deseeded and chopped

4 curry leaves, roughly chopped

1 cup / 200 g canned tomatoes, chopped

1 tsp salt

Cilantro (fresh coriander), to garnish

Method

Prep and cook time: 40 min

1. Boil the potatoes in a large pan of salted water until tender. Drain well and set aside.

2. Heat the butter in a wide skillet and fry the onion until soft but not brown. Add the all the seeds, curcuma (turmeric), garam masala and chili peppers and cook for 2 more minutes.

3. Stir in the curry leaves then add the tomatoes and salt and simmer very gently for about 15 minutes, stirring from time to time, until the sauce is very thick. Add a little water during the cooking if needed to prevent burning.

4. Stir the potatoes into the sauce and garnish with the cilantro (fresh coriander). Serve with boiled rice.

SICHUAN STYLE BEANS WITH GINGER AND GARLIC

Ingredients

2 tbsp vegetable oil

1 lb / 450 g green beans, trimmed and cut into 2 inch / 5-cm lengths

2 garlic cloves, chopped

3 cm / 1-inch piece fresh ginger root, peeled and grated

½ tsp chili paste

1 tbsp light soy sauce

Pinch of sugar

Salt and pepper

Cilantro (fresh coriander) leaves, to garnish

Method

Prep and cook time: 20 min

1. Heat the oil in a large wok or skillet, add the beans and stir-fry for 3 minutes or until they start to soften.

2. Add the garlic, ginger and chili paste and stir-fry for 30 seconds, then stir in the soy sauce, sugar, salt and pepper. Garnish with cilantro (coriander) leaves and serve at once.

BAINGAN BEMISAL

Ingredients

6 small eggplants (aubergines), sliced in half lengthways

6 tbsp vegetable oil

2 onions, chopped

2 garlic cloves, crushed

Thumb-size piece ginger, peeled and finely chopped

1 tsp curcuma (turmeric)

1 tsp ground coriander

1 tsp ground cumin

1 tsp garam masala

1 red bell pepper, deseeded and cut into chunks

1 potato, peeled, cut into chunks and boiled until just tender

Salt and pepper

Sesame seeds, to serve

Method
Prep and cook time: 35 min

1. Heat the oven to 375ºF, (180ºC / Gas Mark 5)

2. Brush the eggplant (aubergine) skins and flesh with a little of the oil and place in a roasting pan. Cover with kitchen foil and bake for about 20 minutes or until the flesh is tender.

3. While the eggplants are cooking, heat the remaining oil in a wide pan and gently cook the onion and garlic until soft but not brown.

4. Add the ginger, curcuma (turmeric), coriander, cumin and garam masala then cook for 2 minutes. Stir in the bell peppers and cooked potato.

5. Cook very gently, stirring from time to time, for 6 minutes or until the bell pepper is tender.

6. Remove the eggplants from the oven and scoop out the flesh from the centers, leaving a wall about ½ inch / 1 cm thick.

7. Roughly chop the eggplant flesh and stir into the onion/spice mixture. Season with salt and pepper and spoon into the hollowed out eggplants.

8. Scatter over the sesame seeds and serve immediately.

SWEET POTATO STICKS WITH SESAME SAUCE

Ingredients

3 tbsp sesame seeds

6 tbsp honey

3 tsp lemon juice

5½ cups / 800 g sweet potatoes, peeled and chopped into ¼-inch / 5 mm strips

Vegetable oil for deep frying

Method

Prep and cook time: 30 min

1. Toast the sesame seeds, stirring constantly, in a dry skillet over medium-high heat until golden brown. Transfer to a plate to cool.

2. In a small saucepan, heat the honey and lemon juice and stir until smooth. Add the toasted sesame seeds and let cool slightly.

3. Heat the oil in a deep fat fryer to 350°F / 180°C.

4. Pat dry the sweet potato sticks with paper towels, then deep-fry in batches in the hot oil for about 4–5 minutes or until golden. Drain on paper towels.

5. Arrange the sweet potato sticks on a plate and drizzle with a little honey and sesame sauce. Serve the rest of the sauce as a dip.

CHINESE SPICED EGGPLANT

Ingredients

4 small eggplants (aubergines)

1 1/3 cups / 300 ml vegetable oil

1 tbsp sugar

2 tbsp rice vinegar

2 tsp soy sauce

2 tbsp rice wine

2 tsp cornstarch (cornflour), mixed to a smooth paste in 1 tbsp water

1 tbsp spicy (hot) bean paste

1 inch / 3 cm piece fresh ginger root, minced

2 cloves garlic, minced

¼ leek, finely chopped

Method

Prep and cook time: 30 min

1. Trim the eggplants (aubergines) and cut each lengthwise into 6 wedges.

2. Heat the oil in a wok or skillet. Add the eggplant in batches and deep-fry for about 3 minutes, until golden brown. Drain on paper towels and keep warm on a plate.

3. In a small bowl, mix the sugar with the vinegar, soy sauce, rice wine and cornstarch (cornflour) paste to make a sauce.

4. Pour off and discard the oil in the wok, leaving behind a thin film. Add the bean paste, ginger and garlic and stir-fry for 30 seconds. Stir in the sauce and 1 tbsp water. Bring to a boil and stir in the leeks.

5. Pour the hot sauce over the eggplant wedges and serve.

SPICED SPINACH WITH CHILI PEPPERS

Ingredients

3 tbsp clarified butter or oil

4 whole red chili peppers

1 onion, finely sliced

1 garlic clove, finely chopped

Thumb-size piece ginger, peeled and finely chopped

1 tsp coriander seeds

1 tsp cumin seeds

1 tsp black mustard seeds

1lb 12 oz / 750 g spinach, washed and roughly chopped

Salt and pepper

Method

Prep and cook time: 20 min

1. Heat the butter in a pan and gently fry the whole red chili peppers for 2 minutes or until just starting to soften. Remove from the pan and set aside.

2. Fry the sliced onion in the pan until soft but not brown then add the garlic, ginger, coriander seeds, cumin seeds and mustard seeds.

3. Cook very gently for 5 minutes then add the spinach. Cover with a lid and cook for 2 minutes or until the spinach is wilted and soft. Season with salt and pepper and serve garnished with the whole chili peppers.

ALOO BEGIN

Ingredients

6 large potatoes, peeled and cut into chunks

½ cup / 125 ml vegetable oil

2 onions, finely chopped

2 garlic cloves, finely chopped

Thumb-size piece ginger, peeled and grated

2 tbsp fennel seeds

1 red chili pepper, deseeded and finely chopped

1 tsp curcuma (turmeric)

1 tsp ground coriander

1 tsp sugar

2 tbsp tomato paste (purée)

2 large eggplants (aubergines), diced

Salt and pepper

To garnish:

3 tbsp oil

1 red bell pepper, deseeded and sliced

1 tbsp chopped cilantro (coriander)

Method

Prep and cook time: 45 min

1. Boil the potatoes in salted water until just tender. Drain well and set aside.

2. Meanwhile, heat the oil in a wide pan and cook the onions very gently until soft but not brown.

3. Add the garlic, ginger, fennel seeds, chili, curcuma (turmeric) and coriander and cook for 2 minutes.

4. Stir in the sugar and tomato paste (purée) then add the eggplant (aubergine) and about a cup of water. Season with salt and pepper and simmer very gently, stirring from time to time, for 20 minutes or until the eggplant is very soft then mash with a fork.

5. Meanwhile, heat the oil for the garnish in a skillet and fry the bell peppers for 5 minutes. Remove from the skillet and set aside.

6. Add the cooked potatoes to the eggplant, cook for 5 more minutes then serve garnished with the bell pepper and cilantro (coriander) leaves.

SPICY GREEN BEANS

Ingredients

2 lb 4 oz / 1 kg green beans, trimmed and cut into 2-inch / 5-cm lengths

Vegetable oil, for deep-frying

2 garlic cloves, minced

2 chili peppers, seeded and chopped

2 scallions (spring onions), finely chopped

1 inch / 3 cm piece fresh ginger root, peeled and grated

1 cup / 100 g canned kidney beans, rinsed and drained

2 tbsp rice wine

2 tbsp fish sauce

Soy sauce, to taste

Method
Prep and cook time: 45 min

1. Heat the oil in a deep fat fryer to 350°F / 180°C. Working in batches, deep-fry the beans until they begin to wrinkle. Drain the beans on paper towels and keep warm.

2. Heat 2 tbsp of the oil in another wok or skillet; add the garlic, chili peppers, scallions (spring onions) and ginger. Stir-fry for 1 minute, then add the kidney beans, 2–3 tbsp water, the rice wine and fish sauce and simmer for 1–2 minutes.

3. Add the green beans and season with soy sauce; heat through and serve at once.

CHINESE BROCCOLI WITH ORANGE

Ingredients

1 head broccoli, stems peeled and cut into small florets

Finely grated zest and juice of 1 orange

2 tsp cornstarch (cornflour)

1 tbsp light soy sauce

½ tsp sugar

2 tbsp olive oil

1 inch / 3 cm piece fresh ginger root, peeled and cut into thin slivers

2 garlic cloves, chopped

1 cup / 100 g bean sprouts

Method

Prep and cook time: 20 min

1. Bring a large pot of water to a boil. Add the broccoli and blanch for 30 seconds; drain in a colander under cold running water to stop the cooking. Drain and set aside.

2. To prepare the sauce, in a small bowl, mix the orange juice and zest with 4 tbsp water, the cornstarch (cornflour), soy sauce and sugar and set aside.

3. Heat the oil in a wok or large skillet; add the ginger and garlic and stir-fry for 10 seconds. Add the broccoli and stir-fry for 2 minutes more. Add the bean sprouts and cook for 1 more minute.

4. Stir the orange sauce mixture into the wok and cook, stirring constantly, until the sauce has thickened and coated the broccoli. Spoon into a serving dish and serve at once.

SPICY EGGPLANT

Ingredients

2 lb 4 oz / 1 kg Thai eggplants
(aubergines)

4–6 fresh red chilies

¼ cup / 60 ml oil

²⁄₃ cup / 150 ml vegetable
broth (stock)

1–1¼ cup / 160–200 g bamboo
shoots, cut into thin strips

Salt and freshly milled pepper

Method

Prep and cook time: 20 min

1. Halve some of the Thai eggplants
(aubergines) and halve the chilies
lengthways. Lightly prick the whole
eggplants several times so that they do
not burst during cooking.

2. Heat the oil in a wok and add the chilies.
Then add the eggplants and fry on all sides
for 3–4 minutes, until lightly browned.

3. Add the broth (stock) and cook for a
further 3–4 minutes, until done, adding
the bamboo shoots after 2 minutes. If the
eggplants are still too firm, cook for up to
5 minutes more.

4. Season to taste with salt and pepper and
serve in bowls.

SAAG ALOO

Ingredients

1 lb 2 oz / 500 g potatoes, peeled and cut into bite-size pieces

1 tbsp oil

1 tsp black mustard seeds

1 onion, finely diced

2 cloves garlic, finely chopped

1 tsp ginger, freshly grated

1 tsp chili powder

2 limes

1 lb 2 oz / 500 g fresh spinach

Method

Prep and cook time: 30 min

1 Parboil the potatoes in salted water for 10 minutes then drain.

2 Heat 1 tsp of the oil in a nonstick skillet and briefly toast the mustard seeds. Add the diced onion, garlic and ginger and fry for 1–2 minutes, stirring constantly. Add the chili powder, potatoes, the juice of 1 lime and a scant ¼ cup / 50 ml water.

3 Put a lid on the pan and cook the potatoes over a low heat for about 15 minutes, take care that the pan does not boil dry. Wash and drain the spinach, add to the pan and mix with the potatoes. Cook for about 3 minutes, until the spinach has wilted.

4 Check the seasoning and serve onto plates. Cut the remaining lime into wedges and add to the dish as a garnish.

INDEX

Oriental noodle bake 334
Oriental salad with shrimp 106
Oyster sauce, chicken and noodles 216

Pad Thai
  with beef 254
  chicken 190
Paneer, lentil curry with 338
Peppers, chicken with red peppers 208
Plum sauce, with pork 166
Pork
  bean curry with pork 158
  with coconut and ginger sauce 152
  curry with fresh herbs 174
  curry with tamarind 162
  fried with vegetables
   and hoisin sauce 170
  with ginger and chili 176
  hot and sour soup 10
  with noodles and vegetables 178
  with plum sauce 166
  ribs with scallions and chilies 172
  roast with vegetables 160
  satay 164
  spare ribs with shitake
   mushrooms 156
  spicy vindaloo 168
  sweet and sour 154
Potatoes
  Aloo Begun 386
  beef curry with potatoes and nuts 266
  Bombay aloo 374
  curry with zucchini
   and cashew nuts 358
  ground lamb, potato and spinach 134
  lentil and potato curry 342
  potato curry soup with chicken 16
  potato pakoras with yogurt sauce 62
  Saag aloo 394
Prawns, spicy king prawns 316
Pumpkin
  shrimp and pumpkin curry 290
  soup with chicken 42
Punjabi style chickpeas 352

Raita
  chicken kebabs 194
  tandoori chicken 234
Red beef curry 260
Red chicken curry 212

Red lentil soup 18
Ribbon noodles with coconut curry
  sauce 364
Rice noodles with cabbage and red
  coconut sauce 348
Roast beef salad 116
Roast duck breast with vegetables 202
Roast duck salad 96
Roast lamb with Indian spices 136
Roast pork with vegetables 160
Rogan josh, lamb 142

Saag aloo 394
Salads
  blackened Indian sticks
   on a bed of salad 186
  chicken with mint leaves 108
  fried fish on mango salad 112
  Indian rice 372
  noodle salad with shrimp 110
  oriental salad with shrimp 106
  roast beef 116
  roast duck 96
  spicy noodle 114
  Thai shrimp and peanut 98
  wakame, water chestnut
   and orange 102
Salmon
  curry with mango 324
  curry soup 28
  diced with soy dip 86
  fillet with coconut curry sauce 306
  steamed with garlic oil 284
  teriyaki salmon with egg noodles 278
Samosas
  lamb 52
  vegetable 54
Scallops
  shrimp and scallop skewers 80
  soup with chili and lemongrass 38
Sea bass steaks with Indian spices 274
Seafood tempura 68
Sesame chicken, with cashews
  and vegetables 242
Sesame sauce, with sweet potato
  sticks 380
Sesame seeds, chicken wings with 90
Shiitake mushrooms
  and noodle soup 26
  spare ribs with 156

Shrimps
  balls 60
  in batter with cashews and rice 322
  curry 280
  fish curry with shrimp 288
  hot and sour soup 40
  and mango curry 304
  nasi goreng 298
  noodle salad with shrimp 110
  noodles with shrimp
   and vegetables 294
   and pumpkin curry 290
   and scallop skewers 80
  sweet potato and shrimp cakes 92
  tiger shrimps Maharaja style 312
  and tomato kebabs with Thai sauce 88
Sichuan beef 250
Sichuan fish, braised 276
Sichuan style beans with ginger
  and garlic 376
Snow peas
  eggplant and snow pea curry 340
  fried fish with ginger, carrot and 320
Sole, with lime sauce 300
Soups
  chicken with almonds 24
  chicken noodle 36
  hot and sour shrimp 40
  miso with vegetables 30
  pumpkin with chicken 42
  red lentil 18
  salmon curry 28
  scallops with chili and lemongrass 38
  shiitake mushroom and noodle 26
  spicy beef 44
  sweetcorn and crab meat 14
  tamarind and coconut 34
Spare ribs with shiitake mushrooms 156
Spiced lamb with chickpeas 144
Spicy beef soup 44
Spicy eggplant 392
Spicy green beans 388
Spicy king prawns 316
Spicy lamb and tomato curry 146
Spicy marinade 120
Spicy noodle salad 114
Spinach
  chicken with spinach
   and zucchini 206
  cod curry with spinach 296

Published by Transatlantic Press

First published in 2011

Transatlantic Press
38 Copthorne Road, Croxley Green, Hertfordshire WD3 4AQ

© Transatlantic Press

Images and Recipes by StockFood © The Food Image Agency

Recipes selected by Marie Clayton

A catalogue record for this book is available from the British Library.

ISBN 978-1-907176-79-1

Printed in China